# Personal Safety & Self-Defense for Real Estate Professionals

By Joe Rosner
Best Defense USA
Joe.rosner@usa.net

### Personal Safety and Self-Defense
Introduction and Overview................................................................................................ 1
Safety and the Bottom Line............................................................................................... 2
Types of Workplace Violence............................................................................................ 3
Warning Signs of Violence................................................................................................ 4
Techno Crimes.................................................................................................................. 5
Reducing the Risk: Plans, Policies & Procedures............................................................. 5
Self-Defense Techniques................................................................................................ 19
Safety and Self-Defense Tools........................................................................................ 30

### Frauds, Scams, Financial Crimes and Identify Theft
Money Laundering in Residential Real Estate................................................................ 37
Real Risks in the Virula World........................................................................................ 38

### Working Safer Everyday
Developing the Safety Habit........................................................................................... 50
Safety Resources............................................................................................................ 50

Closing Thought.............................................................................................................. 51

Case Studies................................................................................................................... 52

**The New Real Estate Safety Book**


**In this book you'll learn:**

- The extent and impact of crime and violence in real estate occupations and associated risk factors
- How plans, policies and procedures can reduce the level of risk
- Safety strategies, tactics and techniques to be used if threatened or attacked
- Simple, effective, self-defense techniques
- The pros and cons of various self-defense tools
- The risks of online threats to your safety, reputation and privacy
- Safety habits and resources

## Introduction

**What does it mean to be safe?** Do you feel safe? Are you safe? You can feel safe even if you're not, and you can be safe and not feel safe. The purpose of this book is to help you learn to be both. After reading this book you will have less fear, be more self confident, be better able to recognize and avoid dangerous people and situations and be better prepared to handle a real or threatened attack if you experience one.

Of course, <u>being</u> safe is essential. Suffering an injury, trauma or even death while providing real estate related services would have a profound, life-altering impact on yourself, your family, your co-workers and even your community. It is just common sense to take all reasonable steps to be as safe as possible. Because even if the likelihood of becoming a victim of crime and/or violence on the job is small (it is probably higher than you may think), the immeasurable loss and suffering that result makes for an unacceptable risk. Remember: Dead agents don't cash commission checks!

At the same time, it is important to feel safe too, because feeling safe is a prerequisite to performing at your best and highest potential. Groundbreaking psychologist, Abraham Maslow, developed his "Hierarchy of Needs"* from studying high achieving people. Maslow said that people had five sets of needs, which occur in a specific order and that you must meet the most basic needs first before it is possible for you to move to your next, more evolved level.

Only the biological requirements needed to stay alive, come before safety. The conclusion is; you cannot excel in the field of real estate if you do not feel safe. Or put another way - Scared real estate agents are less likely to succeed!

**Safety and the Bottom Line**
Pretty much all real estate brokerage managers will say their agents are their most valuable asset. No doubt that is true. And no doubt they mean it when they say it. On the other hand, what other "valuable asset" would they advertise as being left alone, in an unlocked building for four hours? Safety is about people, not ROI, yet there is strong business case for instituting and maintaining safe real estate practices.

1. Crime scene investigation and clean up can close a real estate brokerage for a prolonged period of time. The result can be not only the lack of a well-equipped workspace, but also access to important records.

2. In 1993, seven employees were shot to death at a Brown's Chicken restaurant. Business dropped 35 percent within months of the incident, and the company eventually had to close 100 restaurants in the Chicago area.** Brown's has never recovered and eventually was forced into bankruptcy.
   (Hussain, Rummana (2009-08-10). "After Brown's Chicken massacre: 'No one came'". Chicago Sun-Times)

3. By being an employer of choice, a real estate firm, not only attracts the best people, but also enjoys lower hiring costs. When a firm is well known for a good work environment people proactively seek jobs with it. But if prospective agents and employees think of a tragic incident that happened at a brokerage they will be less likely to look for or accept an opportunity there.

4. Losing a key team member is not only an emotional trauma, there are real costs associated with the accompanying loss of productivity. Even people not directly impacted by being victimized may choose to seek positions elsewhere that they perceive as safer.

**Real Estate Career Opportunities: Rewards and Risks**
Real estate occupations offer a fun, flexible and rewarding career. You can choose your own hours, work location, and even control your income to a large extent. But it is not without its risks. Don't let the risks deter you. Risks can be managed, but first you need to know what they are.

Safety related statistics in real estate occupations exist, but may not be an accurate reflection of the overall safety of the industry. It is widely believed that violence against real estate agents is underreported for a number of different reasons:
♦ Victims may feel they will be blamed. (Well, what was she wearing?)
♦ They may be embarrassed.
♦ Authorities don't always identify and report a victim's occupation.
♦ More than half of ALL violent crimes are not reported to the police according to the US Bureau of Labor Statistics (BLS)

At the same time, statistics don't matter. Whether the odds are one in four or one in four million makes no difference if … you're the one!

♦ The 2015 NAR Member Safety Report found that 96% of their members who responded to the survey report having never been a victim of a crime while working as a real estate professional. The same survey found 40% of real estate professionals (48% of females) have had at least one experience that caused them to fear for their safety. **(Image: NAR 2015 Report Cover)**

♦ In 2014, the most recent statistics available from the BLS, there were 240 non-fatal, violence-related injuries in real estate occupations severe enough to require time off from work. In the same year, there were twenty reported homicide victims who were murdered while working in the real estate field.

♦ Industry experts commonly cite that in an average year between twenty and twenty-five real estate professionals are murdered on the job.

While working in the field of real estate has some unique risks it also shares some of the general risk factors for workplace violence across all career fields. Before looking at these general risk factors let's examine the typology of workplace violence.

# Typology of Workplace Violence

**Workplace Violence Type I: Criminal Intent**
The perpetrator has no relationship with you or your employer. Their only purpose in having an "encounter" with you is to commit a crime, usually robbery or sexual assault. Often, this type of violence is planned ahead of time, but can happen when a criminal spots a "target of opportunity."

Other cases happen when a crime in progress is discovered. A criminal is caught stealing from an open house or breaking into a car and the victim attempts to stop them or even hold them for the police.

In 2014 more than 30 percent of homicides at work were a result of criminal intent.

**Workplace Violence Type II: Customers and Their Families/Friends**
This type of violence results from customers who become disgruntled when a transaction does not meet their expectations. Changing homes is one of the most stressful transitions in people's lives. Under high levels of stress, an otherwise well-behaved person can act out and decide that blame for not getting their "dream house", closing on time or lining up a mortgage, are because of actions (or failures to act) taken by their or the other party's agent.

It can also can begin when a customer develops feelings for, fantasies about or imagines they have a relationship with a real estate professional. Members of the real estate profession often cannot know the background of prospects and customers or be aware of any underlying mental health issues. Nearly 20 per cent of workplace homicides in 2014 resulted from Type II workplace violence.

**Workplace Violence Type III: Lateral or Worker on Worker**
Often, called "Going Postal." This type of violence happens between people who work with each other. Worker on worker fatalities makes up about 15 percent of all workplace homicides in 2014.

**Workplace Violence Type IV: Domestic Violence in the Workplace**
The perpetrator has a personal relationship with an employee and shows up on their job looking to resolve one or more issues. This type of workplace violence accounted for about 7 percent of all workplace homicides in 2014.

 **Type 1: Criminals**

 **Type 2: Customers**

 **Type 3: Employees**

 **Type 4: Related Parties**

## Warning Signs of Potential Violence

**Pre-Incident Indicators of Violence** Be alert for one or more of the following pre-violence indicators. If you see one or more increase your level of vigilance. Use of good judgment is required. The more indications and the greater the level of severity the more concern is called for.
- Co-workers/others fearful, even without specific reasons
- Irrational beliefs or ideas
- Obsessed with weapons and/or acts of violence
- Drastic changes in belief systems
- Displays of unwarranted anger
- Inability to take criticism
- Expresses plan to hurt self or others
- Expresses hopelessness/severe anxiety
- Vandalizes property
- Lacks concern for the safety of others

> **Take all threats seriously! If you see warning signs of violence:**
> - **Alert management immediately**
> - **Mentally prepare for "what if" situations**
> - **Review your safety plan**

## Risk Factors in Real Estate Occupations

*"Because she was just a woman that worked alone -- a rich broker,"* Aaron Lewis, convicted killer of Beverly Carter, when asked why Carter was targeted.

Aaron Lewis is not a criminologist, he just a criminal. Yet, he was easily able to list three of the eight general risk factors for workplace violence. Beverly Carter was a woman. She was working alone, and he thought she was rich.

Law enforcement, OSHA and other authorities have identified the following factors as increasing a person's chances of being a victim of crime and/or violence at work.
1. Working alone or in isolation.
2. Handling or possessing cash or other valuables (or being perceived as doing so.)
3. Working at night and/or early mornings.
4. Being employed in higher crime locations.
5. Having a mobile workplace.
6. Having a workplace with uncontrolled public access.
7. Being female.
8. Working with emotional unstable individuals.

Aaron Lewis

## Reducing the Risk: Plans, Policies & Procedures

**The Number One Way to Reduce Your Risk-** There is one thing people, including those employed in the field of real estate, do that puts them most at risk to be victimized by crime and violence. It's not parking next to white vans. It's not wearing short skirts or low-cut tops. It's not failing to look under their car before getting in. It is <u>choosing not to believe</u> that they could become a victim!

Do you know someone who takes pride in boasting, "This is such a nice area to live, we don't even lock our doors"? People want to believe they're safe. We create an illusion of comfort; a falsely idealized notion that we reside in a world where something bad "can't happen to me." The truth is wishing for something doesn't make it so. Another truth is about a third of home invasions utilize an unlocked door.

Safety is not about being fearful. It doesn't require living your life always worrying about danger. Safety means living in and being aware of, the real world so you can stop worrying and focus on making the most of your life. There is an old saying, "Hope for the best, but prepare for the worst." Not bad advice. Even better, "Prepare for the worst, then go enjoy your life."

**"Myths" About Safety**
Sometimes no advice is better than bad advice. Here a just of few examples of well-intended, but unhelpful advice found in articles, training programs and web pages.

- Don't show properties after dark. Darkness can help criminals hide. But if you work in the Northern United States can you really afford to stop selling at 3:00PM? Instead, it may make more sense to take extra precautions like taking someone with you. For instance, a co-worker, family member or loan officer.

- Using the key fob "Panic Button" to sound your car alarm. In many neighborhoods car alarms are ignored. But if you talk with the neighbors and ask them to call 911 if your alarm sounds then it may work, especially if you let them hear it first.

- Kicking a man in their manly parts. Ask any man when they became concerned about being kicked there. Chances are it was preschool or kindergarten. Men know that's a target and are well prepared to dodge a kick or even grab your foot and throw you to the ground. Even if you succeed it may not disable them and can make them madder and stronger from adrenaline.

- Carry wasp spray for self defense, Even if you're willing to walk around with a can of super bug death in your hand, insecticide may not work fast enough to help. It is hard to aim and does not have a safety. Pepper spray is better.

- Using keys sticking out from between you fingers as a striking tool. This will only work IF you are a skilled puncher and willing to strike at the eyes or trachea of your assailant. Anywhere will only result in a minor scratch or puncture wound.

- Look underneath your car before you get in. An attacker may lie-in-wait there and grab your ankles as you get in! There is an Internet legend about a skinny mugger crawling underneath a car and waiting for the owner to return so he could disable her by slashing her ankle and then assault her. It could happen, but how often? It does not make sense that a criminal would risk getting run over and getting filthy when they can just sneak up between parked cars.

**Office Safety Policies**
Brokerage owners and managers need to take the lead in establishing office wide safety policies and guidelines. There is no better way to make sure your team knows you value them as employees and as people. Broker/Managers should never risk having to live with knowing something tragic happened to one of their people and perhaps they could have done something to prevent it.
Safety is always important. There is no debate about that. Too often it's seen as not very urgent. After all, what are the chances of something happening today or tomorrow or even this month? Not likely, but not zero either.

Let's look at safety another way. Have you ever taken an airline flight that began without a safety briefing? If a flight attendant announced they'll be skipping the safety briefing on this flight because it is almost never needed, you would run off that plane as fast as you could and never fly that airline again. Of course, the flight attendant would be right, the chances of an airline flight having a serious crash are only about one in 11 million. The odds a real estate professional will be the victim of a crime while working are only 1 in 25 and the odds of them finding themselves in a dangerous or threatening situation are 1 in 4. So, does it make any more sense that a Broker/Manager send their team out into the world without having plans, policies and procedures to help keep them safe, especially a regular safety briefing?

Here are some steps to protect real estate agents and brokers.

Creating office safety policies is the first step. It is important not just to have policies, but to make sure the whole team knows about the policies, understands them and follows them. New hires should be furnished with a copy and it should be reviewed in whole or in part at meetings on a regularly scheduled basis.

**Key Steps in Implementing an Office Safety Policy**

1. Ask a reliable employee to volunteer as the office safety co-ordinator. They should be well respected by the team and have access to and the enthusiastic support of top management.

2. Assess the risks faced by team members. This should include:

    ♦ Security at the office during and after business hours

    ♦ Procedures for meeting first time clients

    ♦ Open house safety requirements

    ♦ Social media safety considerations

    ♦ An emergency communications plan

3. Create and implement the safety policies.

4. Regular review and updating of the safety policies.

5. Keep your marketing materials professional. Avoid provocative "calendar style" photographs in advertising, online, brochures, business cards, etc. Tight and low-cut blouses, short skirts and extreme high heels may attract the wrong kind of attention. As we saw in Real Crime Story # 1, predator Matthew Wilson collected business cards and circled photos of female real estate agents in real estate publications and likely planned to target them.

<u>Showing Property Safely</u>

**Know Them Before You Show Them-** If you were not in the real estate business and someone you did not know called and asked you to meet them in a vacant home, would you do it? Probably not! Yet, there is little difference in meeting a new prospect before checking them out. This is not only a good safety measure, it also helps you prioritize your time and even to establish an image as a top professional that they will be lucky to work with.

One of the easiest ways to screen a prospect is to ask if they have secured a mortgage. If yes, get permission to call their Loan Officer and get a copy of their pre-approval. Tell them this will help you to be sure you're showing them the best properties for them and their families and make the best use of your time together. If they don't have a mortgage lined up, tell them you have a great Loan Officer and get the prospect's okay to have the L.O. get in touch. As in before, explain you want be sure you're showing them the best properties for them and their families and make the best use of your time together.

Prospects can also be checked against the Sex Offender Registry. The U.S. Department of Justice's National Sex Offender Public Registry http://goo.gl/lXhnKw is the only publicly accessible national sex offender registry offered by the US Government. If you have a name and a good guess on their age you'll be able to tell if they are listed. Remember not all sex offenders get caught or bother to register as required. James Hole (see Crime Story # 2) was a convicted sexual predator. Although there is no way to be sure, if Anne Nelson had checked him out maybe she would have decided not to go meet with him.

A Sex Offender Registry look up can also be done by entering an address and specifying a radius. Registered sex offenders will then be identified and mapped. Running a location-based search before holding open houses will help you be aware of potential predators in the area. Checking for sex offenders near your office a few times a year is also a good safety measure.

**Caller ID Issues and Concerns**
Caller ID has become an important tool for screening out nuisance calls and verifying where a call originated from. Calls from blocked numbers or labeled as private are not only annoying but may even allow predators to reach out from behind a curtain of anonymity. Of equal or greater concern is the increased use of caller ID spoofing technology, which allows the caller to display a phone number different from that of the telephone from which the call was placed. When done as a prank it is harmless. When used to facilitate a criminal act is can be fatal. On mobile phones there are a number of apps that can reveal the real number calling. For landlines services known as "call traps" are available by monthly subscription.


**Background Checks**
Online background screening companies offer an easy way to check out prospects, vendors and job candidates. However, there are two considerations to be aware of.   1. Make sure you understand the limitations for the type of background check you are ordering. The $20 a month unlimited search deals do have some value but may miss serious criminal histories.  The $40+ searches are better, but ordering one before meeting every prospect is cost prohibitive. 2. Refusing to accept a client due to a failed background check may be breaking the law and face housing discriminating allegations. So be sure you choose a background-screening firm than can help keep you compliant. The safest way to do that is to select a member of the National Professional Background Screeners Association.

Smartphone based solutions, such as Secure Show* can verify the identity of prospects prior to an initial face-to-face meeting. This not the same as a criminal background check, but it does allow you to determine if the person you're going to meet is who they say they are.

*As an example only, no endorsement of any product or service is being made.


**Meeting New Prospects**
It is always safer to meet new prospects at your office. Ask them to let you copy their driver's license and attach it to a completed prospect identification form. Sample Prospect ID and Agent Itinerary Forms are included on the next pages.

## Prospect Identification Form

**This form is designed for your safety and security, along with that of property owners and our agents. We appreciate your consideration and cooperation. All security information is confidential and will not be sold or used for solicitation purposes.**

This information may be subject to verification. Form is to be kept in branch office.

AGENT'S NAME: _____

YOUR NAME(S): _____

HOME ADDRESS: _____

HOME & BUSINESS NUMBERS: _____

IN FROM OUT OF TOWN: _____  LOCAL CONTACT PHONE: _____

LOCAL ADDRESS: _____

I (WE) CAN BE CONTACTED AT THIS LOCATION UNTIL: _____

EMPLOYER: _____  PHONE: _____

Another option is to use your phone to take a picture of the prospects ID and then text or email to another team member, manager or an account established for this purpose.

Be sure the office knows where you are and when you should be expected back. Pilots know that filing an accurate flight plan is the cheapest life insurance available. Should they not land where and when they are expected, a timely search will be launched. Real estate offices should establish a system to track the whereabouts and schedules of agents. This can be a simple paper form, an automated mobile phone tracking app or just a quick text or email detailing where you're going and when you expect to be back. Make a habit of letting your team know your schedule so you're never wishing someone knows where you are should you need help.

Real estate agents and brokers should make sure that their emergency contacts list, their description and photo as well as the make, model, color and license plate number of their vehicles(s) are kept on file. Ideally, this information is stored on a secure intranet to permit fast, remote access after hours.

Before mobile phones became common, some parents would leave an alarm clock, set for their teen child's curfew, outside their bedroom door. If the child didn't make it home and shut it off on time, they didn't get the car keys the following weekend. Consider setting up a similar system with your manager, partner, admin or spouse so if you fail to return from an appointment promptly they can take appropriate actions.

---

### Agent Itinerary Form

**This form is designed for your safety and security. Please leave the completed form with the receptionist, along with your showing itinerary information.**

AGENT: _____     DATE: _____

CUSTOMER/CLIENT NAME(S): _____

☐ Personal Identification Form attached.

☐ Personal Identification Form already on file with:

ANTICIPATED TIME OF RETURN TO OFFICE: _____     ☐ AM     ☐ PM

MY CONTACT PHONE WHILE SHOWING PROPERTY: _____

COMMENTS: _____

This National Association of Realtors form can be downloaded at www.realtor.org

**Encounters With Dogs**

With an estimated seventy to eighty million dogs in the United States it is inevitable you will encounter them while showing homes or meeting prospects. Most dogs are friendly or at least not aggressive. But all dogs will bite under the right circumstances. At the same time almost all dog bites can be prevented.

The first step in avoiding a dog bite is to be polite and respect the dog's personal space. Never advance towards an unfamiliar dog, particularly if it is tied up or locked in a fenced yard. Never pet a dog until you let them see and sniff you first.

Any dog that doesn't know you may see you as a threat coming to harm him and his family. When a dog is sleeping, eating its food, chewing on a toy or taking care of puppies it is much more likely to have strong protective feelings and become aggressive. Extra caution should be exercised around strange dogs.

Maintain a safe amount of distance between yourself and a dog if you see a dog giving off warning signs. If a dog is feeling stressed or feels it needs to protect itself, family or territory it will give of indications including--

- Body tensed
- Tail stiff or held up high
- Ears flattened back against its head
- Nose is pulled back and wrinkled
- Lips are pulled back to show teeth
- The hair along his neck and spine is raised
- His body is tense
- He is growling or snarling
- Shows you "whale eyes" (Eyes rolled so the whites are visible.)
- Flicking its tongue
- Hard stare
- Backing away
- Excessive yawning

Dog will often view running away as prey behavior. Many dog breeds are hard-wired to chase and bring down prey. So when you're creating space between yourself and a dog who is exhibiting aggression, never turn and run away. A dog's natural instinct will almost always be to chase you.

If you are approached or encounter a dog that seems ready to attack-

- Control your impulse to scream and run away.
- Turning sideways to the dog will reduce its stress level and keep them from biting your most sensitive body areas.
- Avoid direct eye contact with the dog.
- Say "No" or "Go Home" in a firm deep voice.
- Stay still with your hands at your sides, and avoid eye contact with the dog.
- Slowly, back away.
- If you are carrying pepper spray get it in your hand, ready to use. If the dog seems to be working its self up for an attack, sometimes spraying pepper spray between you and the dog will make it change its mind. But when under attack or if you have any doubts, spray the dog directly in its face. Be aware pepper spray may not work on trained attack dogs and may take a second or to become effective.

If facing an incipient or actual attack, put a barrier between yourself and the dog. Bicycle, jackets, briefcases may be used to shield you. Should the dog knock you down or if you just trip, get into a fetal position with your hands over your ears and remain still. Do not to scream or roll around.

## Showing Vacant Property

Foreclosures and REO properties can offer some great opportunities. Always keep in mind unoccupied homes and other buildings have a higher risk level than occupied properties. These risks include:

1. Property listed as vacant is more likely to attract undesirable people and activities.
2. Squatters may illegally move in.
3. Drug users and dealers may set up "shooting galleries" to sell and use drugs out of public view.
4. Meth labs are often found in empty houses.
5. Evicted, former occupants have been known to return seeking to commit vandalism and other crimes.
6. Thieves looking to steal copper wire, piping and other items can be surprised.
7. Electricity may be shut off making lighting a safety issue.
8. Some of the entry doors may be blocked or secured with plywood, limiting your emergency exits.
9. Alarm systems and telephones will probably be shut off, reducing the means of getting help.
10. Predators may seek to lure unsuspecting real estate salespeople to empty homes to be victimized.

Vacant property is inherently risky, but can be made less risky with safety procedures like:

- Never listing a property as vacant.
- Do not show empty properties by yourself.
- Do not enter a vacant building without a good flashlight. Smartphone flashlight apps should not be relied upon, as they can quickly deplete the phone's battery and are frequently used to install malware. Knock on the neighbor's doors. Introduce yourself and ask if they have seen any activity around the property in question. Activating your car's alarm via the key fob is not reliable, especially in areas where car alarms are commonly ignored. Letting the neighbors know you intend to set off the alarm in an emergency and asking they then call 911 may add a layer of security.
- Walk around the home's perimeter. Look for signs of entry, such as footprints near windows or doors that have been forced open. Be alert for any signs that home is in use including garbage, yard used as a toilet, drug paraphernalia or tampering with utility meters.
- Knock loudly and wait for a moment before opening the door.
- Stand to the side of the door, when opened and loudly announce yourself and your intentions. For example: *"I'm a real estate agent. I'm here to show the house. Anybody here?"*
- Upon entering, stand still for a moment and listen. Do you hear anyone, smell food, or notice any signs that property may not be vacant? When in doubt, LEAVE!
- Pay attention to piles of clothing/blankets, food containers, etc.
- Consider asking the seller to install an alarm system. While all systems require a source of electric power, many newer units do not require a telephone landline or need sensors to be hardwired. Many of these systems can be monitored and operated with a smartphone app.

If you encounter an unauthorized occupant, don't overreact. Take a slow breath. Act like nothing is wrong. Explain you thought the home was empty and leave immediately. Get to your car, lock the door and drive to a safe location.

The emerging crime of rental fraud* increases the likelihood of encountering an individual who believes they have signed a lease, paid a deposit and some rent and therefore are entitled to live in the home. Foreclosed properties may still have former owners living in them. Perhaps they are slow to bow to the inevitable or there have been cases where the bank failed to notify the former owner. In both these types of situations you may be asked to resolve the issue. The fraud victim or the soon-to-be–evicted former owner may well be agitated and angry and try to scapegoat you. Don't argue or explain. Just politely explain there is nothing you can do and leave as quickly as you can.

*In this rapidly growing crime scheme Craiglist and similar Internet sites are being used to defraud would-be renters into signing a lease and paying a deposit on an unoccupied property.

### Keeping Your Sellers Safe

Selling their home in not an everyday event for most people. They are relying on your expertise in selling the property for a good price and in good time. Helping protect your client during the sales process is both an obligation and a good business practice. Don't be concerned that you will be creating fear or causing them to not list with you. Most people will appreciate your professional concern.

After completing the listing agreement take some time to consult with the seller and their family. Explain that it is their responsibility to help with security during the sales process. Sellers should be counseled to--

1. Secure any small, pocketable valuables before open houses and showing. This used to mean cash, jewelry and collectibles. But in the last few years criminals have shown up at an open house looking to steal pharmaceuticals. (Reducing clutter always helps stage a home anyway.) Extra keys should be secured as well.

2. Homeowner should also be warned to secure anything that could be used to commit identity theft against them. Banks and credit card statements, utility bills, checkbooks, planner, calendars and other documents are obvious ID Theft fodder. Also, unsecured computers, tablets, smartphones, or USB drives add risk. That is not all. Family trees on the wall can give away birthdays and maiden names, commonly exploited by fraudsters. Certificates, diplomas and awards can contain personally identifiable information. Think like a crook!

3. Don't forget to explain it is important they never allow anyone in to look at the house without an appointment. Criminals may pose as interested buyers or real estate agents and aggressively seek to see the home. Stress that they must always err on the side of safety and call you or your office if any doubts exist.

4. Ask that they walk through the home after every showing and open house looking for any missing items and checking that doors and windows have not be unlocked or tampered with.

5. This is also a good time to ask them about their alarm system if they have one, especially if you'll be holding an open house. Make sure you know if it is monitored and how to arm and disarm it. Also learn to use the panic buttons. Most systems have a feature called "chimes." Turning the chimes on will sound an alert if an exit door is opened.

6. Homeowners should make sure all firearms, other weapons and hazardous items are stored securely.

7. Clients need to understand you are taking safety precautions, and will check and lock the home's doors and windows before leaving. It is also important that they too check all locks and look around for missing items right away after every open house and showing.

8. If the property is going to be empty for a length of time place signs inside and outside warning that *"This property is not for rent!"*, in order to help prevent scammers from fraudulently renting it out.

## Open House & Model Home Safety

Some real estate professionals have chosen to stop conducting open houses. They feel that the safety concerns override any benefit. Others note that sales do result at open houses from prospects that might not be able to set an appointment or are just driving by. Many have found open houses are a good way to meet people who have or will soon have a property they need to sell. Of course, there are real safety concerns but they can be reduced and mitigated.

### Open house safety tactics:

1. Don't go alone! Even if the only person you can get to go to the open house is your grandmother you'll be safer for having another set of eyes and ears with you. Who might you ask to come with you? Co-workers, especially new agents. Loan Officers often are happy to come along as they know open houses are great for meeting people who will need a mortgage soon. Insurance Agents may also be willing to sit with you, but only if asked. Friends and family, too.

2. Allow enough time before an open house to meet the neighbors. Grab some business cards and knock on all the doors, on both sides of the street, up and down the block. Introduce yourself with a script like this one. *"Hi, my name is Joe. I'm a real estate agent and I'm holding an open house at the Young's house across the way. I wanted to give you my business card, my cell phone number is on it, and ask that if you see anything going on in the neighborhood you call and give me a heads up."* Most people want to help others and will agree. (Marketing tip: Always ask if they know anyone looking to move into the area.)

3. Walk through the house to locate all of the exits. You do this when get on an airliner and you should do it before open houses, too. After all, an emergency is not the best time to be figuring out your escape route.

4. If there is a basement, check your phone signal ahead of time, just in case. It is best not to go back down there until the open house is over. If asked, state that you need to remain on the first floor as more people are expected.

5. Make showing proper identification a condition of entry. Don't kid yourself, people who can't or won't show you an ID are not going to buy the house. By insisting on proper identification you will NEVER LOSE A SALE and you may save a lot of grief. You may find it easier to ask if you print up a sign and place it next to your sign-in list or device. Nothing elaborate is required. Just a simple notice.

6. Make a point of positioning yourself between any prospects and an exit at all times. If you decide you need to flee it will be harder to stop you. Be particularly careful in any space with only one way in and out. Encourage people to lead the way, *"I'll follow you, the master bedroom is upstairs."*

7. Keep your hands free. Lock your purse in the car.

8. Carry your pepper spray or self-defense tool of your choice, where it is both concealed and easily accessible. Clip it on your belt or waistband if you're wearing an untucked shirt, attach it to an elastic bracelet under your sleeve or stick it in your boots or socks.

9. Know that everyone may not have left at the end of an open house. Check all of the rooms prior to locking the doors. Be ready in case you suddenly need to flee or defend yourself.

10. Consider getting a real or fake video security system and/or post a warning sign that the premises are under video surveillance.

11. Know who is coming and going. If the home is equipped with an alarm system ask the homeowner how to turn on the door chime so you will be alerted when an entry door is opened. If no security alarm system is installed consider hanging bells or a doorknob alarm on entry doors to warn when doors are opened.

12. If by yourself, lock all entry doors and admit people when they knock or ring the doorbell.

13. Be aware of couples or groups who may have one person distract you while the other steals items or commits other crimes. The greatest risk for this type of activity occurs at the last hour of the open house.

**Commercial Property Safety**

Commercial properties present many of the same risk factors as residential and a few special concerns as well. Properties may be more isolated, unfinished and have fewer people around. Before meeting a prospect at a commercial building consider taking the following steps:

- Determine the cast of characters. Who is expected and authorized to be there? Construction crew, utility workers, etc.? Should you find anyone you don't know for sure to be authorized, leave and call for help.

- Learn what security measures are in place. Alarms? Video security? Guards?

- Make sure your whereabouts and expected time of return have been provided to a reliable, trusted colleague.

- As with residential prospects, make it a policy to meet prospective tenants at your office first. Establish their bonafides before going off alone with them.

**Listing Appointment Safety**

Running off to give selling presentations every time the phone rings puts your safety at higher risk and usually doesn't make good business sense either. Some call this "ring and run" real estate. Taking a small amount of time to qualify a lead will make you safer.

- Ask the prospect where they heard about you? Be aware predators may try to lure you to a place they can victimize you.

- Check the address to determine who owns it.

- Run the prospect's name and the address through the Sex Offender Register.

- If you have the capability to run a criminal background check, do so. Check state and local law enforcement websites that list current and former inmates.

- If the local police have a crime map online check the address there, too.

- Lastly, make sure someone knows where you're going and when to expect you back.

## Safety at the Office

The safety issues inherent in meeting prospects alone in vacant, sometimes isolated, properties are rather obvious. The safety risks at many real estate offices may not be as apparent, but are just as real.

### Office Safety Survey

1. How safe overall is the neighborhood where your office is located? If you don't know Google the office's zip code and "crime map.'

2. Doors, locks and frames should be closely examined.

    - Is the door made of steel, fiberglass or other material strong enough to withstand not to break apart if repeatedly kicked or smashed with a heavy object?

    - Expensive locks make for cheap insurance. If a lock costs less than $150, chances are it can be opened with a bump key or lock pick quickly and easily.

    - Is the frame strong and stiff enough that it cannot be spread open with a pry bar or similar tool to let the lock bolt slip out of the jamb and the door to open?

    - How deep into the doorjamb does the bolt extend? If it is less than a full half inch it may be pried out to open the still locked door.

    - If your doorframe is made of wood, is there a reinforced, high security strike plate installed? Wooden doorframes are most often made from white or yellow pine and will easily break with a good kick.

3. Key distribution should be recorded so you can track who has them. Employees should be required to turn in their keys when they leave the business.

4. A Master key or one key for both outside doors and inside offices is convenient, but makes burglary a simple matter. It's a good idea to code keys so only the employees know which locks they fit.

5. Do associates work alone, especially at off-hours?

6. Is there a working alarm system? *

7. Is there an alarm system or door chime to sound an alert when people come and go?

8. Do you have a decent quality video security?

9. Are there "panic" buttons at the front desk and other accessible places?

10. Are there any nearby businesses, such as bars, that may increase your risks?

11. Is the parking lot well lit and without potential hiding places?

12. Do you have a "safe room" inside the office where you can lock the door and "shelter in place"?

13. Do phone lines enter the building in a secure manner or do they run through an unsecured cabinet at the back of the building?

    *Today's security alarm systems are more than just burglar alarms. They can operate HVAC, lights, illuminated signs and office equipment as well as lock and unlock doors. These functions can be controlled via smartphone or in response to events, for instance turning on lights when doors are opened or lowering the heat at night. Real estate office managers can track who is coming and going and when, or check to see all the windows are closed.

**Auto Safety**
If you're like many real estate salespeople your main office is really your car. And if you're like most American's you rate your driving skills as above average. In fact, a number of studies have found that up to 93 percent of US drivers rate their driving skills as "above average." (Acta Psychologica Volume 47, Issue 2, February 1981, Pages 143–148) Statistically we know that at least forty-three percent of them have to be wrong, which means the reality is that most of us think we are better drivers than we really are. Over confidence can put you at risk.

So how good a driver are you? An honest self-evaluation can help you understand how proficient a driver you are and possibly protect you from a serious accident.

How close to the posted speed limit do you drive? Driving must faster or slower increases the chance you'll have an accident.

When you see a traffic signal change to yellow do you speed up, slam on the brakes or make a decision based on your speed, and distance to the light? Slamming on the brakes can cause a rear end accident. Zooming through a yellow light as it goes to red increases the probability drivers from the cross street will be in the intersection. The best drivers choose a Go/No Go decision point as they approach a traffic-controlled intersection that allows for enough distance to come to a smooth stop. If they are beyond the decision point they continue through the intersection. If the light changes before they reach the decision point they continue on through the intersection.

Do you ever use your cell phone while driving? Talking on a hands-free cellular device still increases your risk, nearly as much as making a call with a handheld phone, because of the level of distraction involved. Paying attention to the phone conversation, regardless if the phone is hands-free or handheld may keep you from recognizing hazards. It would be best to never drive and talk on the phone at the same time. But at the very least, make a decision to only talk on the phone when traffic, weather, visibility and other driving conditions are perfect or close to perfect.

If you encounter another driver who cuts you off or otherwise drives in a rude manner, do you tap your brakes, make an obscene gesture or just focus on your driving? Stupid drivers, whether tailgating or engaging in other unsafe driving are unlikely to change their driving habits based on anything you do or say. It is best just to ignore the behavior, let them pass and go about your business. Or just report them to 911.

Do you always use your turn signals before changing lanes and making turns? Using your turn indicators communicates your intentions to the drivers around you. Not only is this a courteous way to help prevent road rage incidents, it may prevent all the headaches, hassles and involvement in even the smallest fender bender.

Before going to a social event where alcohol is served do you have a plan to stay safe and sober? Determine in advance how many drinks you'll have based on your age, weight, when you last ate and how alcohol affects you. When in doubt just get a Uber, Lyft or Sidecar ride.

Do you maintain at least a three-second interval between your car and the car you are following? At fifty-five miles per hour your car is covering eighty-one feet per second. An exceptional driver needs a minimum of three quarters of a second just to see and recognize the car in front of them is stopping and an average driver will need 2.3 seconds. Increase the interval in bad weather, at night or when you feel tired.

Take a moment to review these safe-driving tips.

- Maintain your car as if your life depends on it, because truly it might. Brakes, lights and wipers should be inspected on a regular basis, but also any maintenance item that could result in a breakdown at the worst possible time.

- Make sure you have a spare tire and a jack and know how to use them.

- Fill the tank when the gauge reads ¼ full and you will never run out of gas.

- Keep <u>two</u> phone chargers in the car.

- Keep a pepper spray in a concealed, but easily accessible place. Or attach it to your keys with a quick release so that it dangles where you can grab it quickly.

- If you are driving through an area where you have safety concerns-

  - Try not to come to a complete stop at traffic lights or elsewhere. Slowing down in advance and keeping your speed to a crawl makes it much more difficult for a criminal to approach your car and attack.

  - To make sure you have maneuvering room to drive off if attacked or threatened, leave one or more car lengths between your car and the car ahead when driving in traffic jams or stopping.

- If you think you are being followed, make three left turns. If the vehicle of concern is still behind you, then you are being followed.

- Using ear buds or hands free function on your phone make sense and is the law in many states. However, the distraction the phone creates takes your attention away from your driving. Distracted driving can double or triple your reaction time.

- Never text while driving. Pull over or wait until you're stopped at a light.

- Always take your own vehicle. Don't ride in the prospect's vehicle.

- Road rage occurs when a driver becomes irrational and loses their self-control. Never leave your vehicle to interact with a rage-impaired driver. Drive carefully, stay in the public view and call 911 if you feel threatened.

- Always take your car when touring properties with a prospect. Never ride in theirs unless you know them well. It is too easy for a predator to conceal weapons, restraints and other items they intend to use against you in their vehicle.


**<u>Parking Lot and Garage Safety</u>**
Many criminals target people, especially women, in parking lots. Frequent news stories document incidents of crime including theft, vandalism, and violent attacks occurring in parking garages and lots. The National Crime Victimization Survey conducted by the Bureau of Justice Statistics, found more than 1 in 10 property crimes including motor vehicle theft and property theft occur in parking lots or garages. Even more alarming, the survey reported that 7.3% of all violent crimes occur in parking facilities. Some industry experts believe that as many as 40 percent of rapes and assaults take place in parking lots.

Parking safety tips to know include:

- If you have a sign with your name on it or vanity license plate, be aware a criminal may call you by your name to lower your guard while approaching you.

- Make a habit of always locking your doors and starting your engine as soon as you enter your car.

- Avoid parking near places that may offer concealment, like bushes or other landscape features. Also larger vehicles can screen you and your car from other people.

- Be sure to park where there will be good lighting when you return. In many parts of the country, from November through April, you can leave your car in daylight only to return at 4:00 to find it is parked in a dark and shadowy place.

- Make a 360 degree scan of the parking lot before unlocking the doors and exiting your vehicle and upon your return. If you see anyone or anything that cause you concern, move your car, call for an escort or take other appropriate steps to be safe. Don't just look for people walking or standing around, check to see if vehicles are occupied too.

- Do not use parking garage stairs or elevators when alone. Walk up the ramp, staying far enough from parked cars to prevent an attacker from jumping out at you.

- Be aware that criminals may attempt to "test" or distract you as you walk to and from your car. Criminals test potential victims by asking them a question and gauging their level of awareness, self-confidence and general suitability as a victim. They may ask for directions, the time or for money.

**Summary**

There is no need to live in fear. Fear limits the quality of life. Astronaut John Glenn was asked if he was scared before launching into orbit in his Mercury space capsule. "No," he replied, "But I do have some creative apprehension." You too might want to engage in creative apprehension. Rather than being fearful, instead look for potential risks, and ask *"What could go wrong here and what will I do if it does?"*

Think like a criminal. Walk around the outside of your office looking for vulnerabilities, lighting, places of concealment, etc. Enter the office and try and get inside unnoticed. Criminals choose victims who appear unaware, un-alert and unprepared. They look for people who appear to lack confidence and will submit without resisting. Be aware of how you look and what "vibe' you're giving off.

Keep in mind that employing safety strategies, tactics and techniques may be keeping you safe even if there is no clear sign that it is working. After all, you probably won't know when a criminal chooses not to select you as a victim.

## Stop and Read This Before Continuing!

The author, the publisher, their successors, assignees, affiliates, the author of this course and book and all other parties involved in the creation, publishing and distribution of this course are not responsible in any manner whatsoever for any injury, harm or loss caused by the application or use of any of the information and instructions included in this work. This includes but is not limited to any and all physical injuries, emotional stress or trauma, loss of property or other negative outcome resulting from the methods and practices described in this course or by the failure of these methods to protect any person from harm.

YOU must carefully consider YOUR emotional, temperamental and physical characteristics and limitations and use your best, considered judgement before proceeding to teach, practice and apply the methods and techniques provided in this course. In the event that any doubt, whatsoever, exists regarding the suitability of any part of this book, err on the side of caution.

Any reading or use of this material constitutes a Waiver of Liability to the author, publisher and all others involved in the creation, publishing and distribution of this instructional book. You are 100% responsible.

**Before learning these self defense techniques please be aware of the following:**

1. Never choose self-defense as an option. Self-defense is for when no other choice is possible. Even black belts lose fights and you may, too. There are no guarantees. Think about self-defense the same way that you think about airbags in your car. Do want them there if needed? Yes, of course. Are you looking for an opportunity to use your airbags? Of course not! You'd never be driving along and think- "Look, I'm about to have a traffic accident. I could swerve or brake, but what the heck, I have airbags." The same holds true for self-defense. It is only to be used as a last resort.

2. Self-defense has only one single purpose, only. To escape to a safe place where you can get help. It is NOT for punishing the person who attacked you.

3. Self-defense is ALWAYS done with maximum power and effort right from the start. It is not implemented gently and ratcheted up to an effective level.

4. Use your strong parts against the attacker's weak parts, e.g., your body weight and biceps against their hand grip.

5. Use your soft parts against their hard parts and your hard parts against their soft parts, e.g., head butting to the nose.

6. Stay calm and breathe long, deep breaths.

7. Never give up! Try something. If it doesn't work, try something else. As long as you're conscious you have a chance.

Practice each of these techniques at half speed and gradually move faster as your skills develop. ALWAYS keep in mind the physical and psychological limitations of yourself and your partner, avoiding any movements that create discomfort. You and your partner should make each other aware of any pre-existing injuries, conditions or limitations. No hard punches or kicks should be used against each other unless adequate safety gear, including padding, is used, and then with qualified, professional instruction.

<u>**REMEMBER!**</u> If all they want is money, jewelry, your car or other property, give it up. Possessions can be replaced. Let it go and file and insurance claim. Use self-defense only when violence is unavoidable or they want to restrain or relocate you and fleeing is not an option.

## Self-Defense Techniques

**First Step:** What is the simplest, most reliable, most effective self-defense technique? Running away! You cannot be the victim of violence if you are not at the scene of the crime. So run away, drive away, get back on your bike and ride away, flee, depart, vamoose.

**Second Step:** Get help, call 911, contact your office, trigger a fire or security alarm or yell.

What should you yell to get help? Many people, including some crime prevention instructors, may suggest yelling "FIRE!" if you are being attacked. This is because there have been a number of incidents in which victims who needed help received none despite a large number of people being aware of the situation and doing nothing. The Kitty Genovese case is probably the best known of these but this type of incident does seem to occur a few times a year. Yet, the reason for this is well known. It is called "the bystander effect" and comes down to two main principals:

1. The more people who know you need help the less likely it is that any individual will get involved and help you. Everyone may think that with so many witnesses someone else will step in to help so they don't need to.
2. People tend to echo bad information. Bystanders monitor the reactions of other people in emergency situations to see if other people think that it is necessary to intervene. If they see no strong reaction from others they may believe this lack of reaction indicates that this is not an emergency.

   In a Columbia University experiment conducted in 1968, students were seated in a room either by themselves or with two or three other strangers and instructed to complete a questionnaire. Shortly after the students began their task, the experimentation team would pump smoke into the room though a wall vent, simulating a fire. Students working by themselves would typically notice and react to the smoke in five seconds or less. Students working in groups took twenty or more seconds to react.

**Formula for Breaking Through the Bystander Effect**
The formula is Attention, Problem, Solution. For example: *"Help! I'm being attacked! Call 911!"* It can be made even more effective if you single out a person specifically for instance: *"You in the blue jacket! Help! I'm being attacked! Call 911!"*

**Third Step:** Shelter in place. Lock yourself in a secure room or hide in, under or behind and large object. If an inward opening door does not have a lock or you don't have the key to lock it, sit on the floor with your feet against the door and lock your knees

**Fourth Step:** Talk your way out of danger. This not reliable but may work or at least buy you time to think. Anyone willing to rob or attack you can't be trusted. So don't believe an attacker's promises. Do not beg nor show fear as that can cause an assailant to become "drunk" with power and more violent. Reasoning with a criminal or person with a mental defect is unlikely to succeed as they have different values than you and may have a completely different reality, too. Tactics for talking your way out include-

- Pretend to be onboard with the attacker's plan. *"I like sex too. But can we go somewhere more comfortable?"* This may provide you an opportunity to escape or get him to drop his guard to better facilitate your sudden attack.

- Gross him out. Urinate, defecate, pick your nose, drool, or pretend to be sick by gagging and/or vomiting.

- Attempt to make him fearful with statements along the lines of- *"I'm expecting more people any moment. That's my husband's truck now, "Hey Frank, over here!", or "That's a police surveillance camera."*

- If you think you're dealing with a deranged person or with an enraged, irrational person, make soothing helpful statements such as- *"I think I understand why your upset. What would you like me to do? "*

**Fifth Step:** Defend yourself. Only as a last resort when you have no other options.

### Physical Self-Defense

### Self-Defense Stance

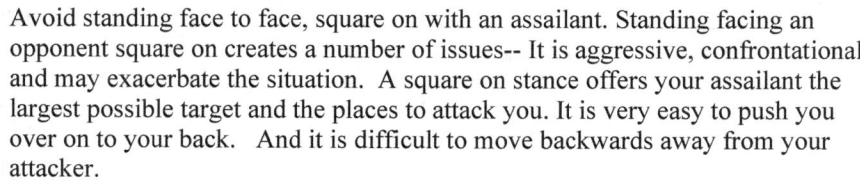

If you find yourself facing an angry, agitated, mentally unbalanced individual or a criminal attacker your stance can make a big difference in keeping you safer.

Avoid standing face to face, square on with an assailant. Standing facing an opponent square on creates a number of issues-- It is aggressive, confrontational and may exacerbate the situation. A square on stance offers your assailant the largest possible target and the places to attack you. It is very easy to push you over on to your back. And it is difficult to move backwards away from your attacker.

1. Your strongest or dominant shoulder is pointed at the other person, with your feet a little wider than shoulder width. Raise your front hand, the one nearest the attacker, to eye level. Your arm should be extended about eighty percent, leaving only a small bend in your elbow. Hands are open, fingers together. Use your front hand and arm to perform most of the active blocking.

2. Your rear hand is placed in front of chest, about four to six inches in front of your chin to protect your face and throat. Hands are open, fingers together.

3. Yell **"Back Off!"** While "snapping" into the stance.

4. Footwork: Pivot on front foot always pointing front shoulder at the attacker. Switch hand positions and turning head reverses the stance. To move forward:
    **A.** Slide front foot, first.
    **B.** Back foot, second.

Backwards is opposite: slide rear foot back first, then your front foot.

**Active Blocking**
Not getting hit, or at least not getting hit hard or in a sensitive spot, is the goal of blocking. Practice blocking with a partner. Partner "A" assumes the self-defense stance and practices blocking, primarily with their front hand. Partner "B" visualizes a clock around Partner "A's" face. Then Partner "B" reaches out to TOUCH, not hit, slap or punch their partner. Start slow and build speed as skills are improved. After a few practice rounds change to reaching out in a random pattern. Switch back and forth between partners.

Pointers for More Effective Blocking
1. Practice gently so as not hurt your partner. But in actual use block HARD,
2. Always bring your hand back to the center. Don't fall for fakes intended to keep your hand out away from your centerline.

3. Blocking can be done with any part of the hand or arm. Blocking with the bony protrusion found on the pinky side of your hand where it meets your wrist is particularly effective.
4. Blocking towards your opponent's center makes it harder for them to hit you with their other hand.
5. Blocking will only work for a limited time. Its purpose is to keep you from being hurt while planning your next move.

### Blocking Kicks

The most common type of kick in a street encounter is a front, football, style kick. This can be blocked from your self-defense stance by simply lifting your front foot up high. Use the bottom of your foot or the outside edge to block the shin of the kicking leg.

### Passive Blocking

Should you find yourself temporarily unable to defend yourself due to being stunned by a blow, panic or an overwhelming "blitz" attack, you'll need to take steps to protect yourself long enough to make a new plan. Use your elbows to form a cage around your face and neck. Place your hands on your ears and your elbows together in front of your nose.

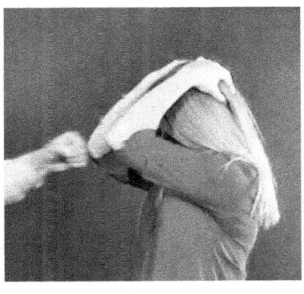

### Stomp Kick

From the self-defense stance, take a sidestep towards the attacker to get close and then bring your nearest knee up high. Slam your foot down on top of their foot at a 90-degree angle, as close to their ankle as you can. Immediately step back away and to one side.

A stomp kick is the most powerful kick you can do. It uses the largest muscle you have, your quadriceps, plus your body weight. Even a very small person can disable a large, strong aggressor with a well-delivered stomp kick because it will damage the bones in the foot called phalanges and the longer metatarsals. Once these bones are bruised or broken the attacker will be in pain and have a greatly reduced ability to chase you. DO NOT STAY AND TRY TO LAND MORE KICKS! Get to a safe place and call 911.

**Escape from Single Hand Wrist Grab**
When an aggressor grabs your wrist, using only a single hand, take these steps:

1. Turn your wrist so the narrow, thumb edge of your wrist lines up with the attacker's thumb and forefinger.

2. Push your own elbow towards the attacker's knuckles to "lever" your wrist free. Bring your other hand over to help if extra strength is needed.

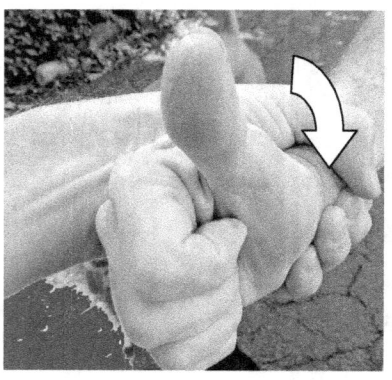
Rotate wrist to thumb and forefinger.

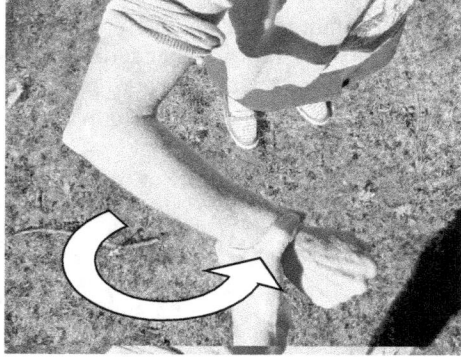
Lever elbow inward.

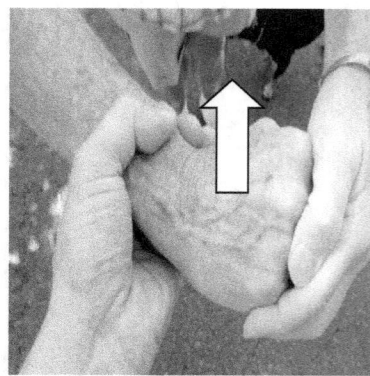
Use your helper hand to pull.

**Escape From Two Handed Wrist Grab**
Should an assailant grab one or both of your wrists with both of their hands, perform the following actions:

1. Clasp your hands together. If an assailant's two hands are on one of your wrists reach over the top to clasp your hand that is being held.
2. Quickly shove down.
3. Step back and pull your hand up by your ears.

Always pull to the ear, **not** to your chest, over your head or face.

Push down hard!

Swing hands to ear and

**Escape from a Choke**

If someone has their hands around your throat, from the front or rear, you can escape by:

1. Raising both hands as high up as you can.

2. Simultaneously step back and turn/twist away.

Raise your hands up on the OUTSIDE of the attacker's arms.

Turn 180 degrees with your feet and upper body, then run to a safe place and get help.

**Defense against a front bear hug** will depend on whether or not you have an arm free. If yes, grab your spray, aim and fire. If you do not have a free arm, drive one of your knuckles as hard as you can into the attacker's lowest rib.

Punch your knuckles into lowest rib and grind.

**Defense against a rear bear hug** can be done with one of the following methods. Drop your weight down and then spring back up driving the top of your head into the assailant's chin. Stomp on their feet. Or reach back to their groin, grab hard, yank and twist.

To protect yourself against being thrown to the ground, hook one of your feet behind the opponent's lower calf.

**Defense From the Ground** If knocked to the ground you must prepare to defend yourself as fast as possible. If you cannot get back on your feet quickly, sit up, and use your feet and hands to spin about, keeping your feet between yourself and the person of concern. If you have and can reach your pepper spray hold it up, aim and fire if a clear opportunity is presented.

**STOMP KICK:** Position yourself sideways to the assailant and take a sidestep towards them while bringing your nearest knee up high. Slam your foot down on their foot at a 90-degree angle, as close to their ankle as you can. Immediately step back away and to one side.

**STEP & PUSH:** This technique is very similar to the stomp kick, but used when you need to control somebody yet wish to avoid injuring them. For example, a friend who had too much to drink or a person suffering dementia. Again, slide in with a side step, quickly, but gently, put your foot on top of theirs with enough of your weight to hold it firm. Then give them a firm shove backwards. They will lose their balance and fall on their back.

**PASSIVE BLOCKING:** Should you find yourself temporarily unable to defend yourself due to being stunned by a blow, panic or an overwhelming "blitz" attack, you'll need to take steps to protect yourself long enough to make a new plan. Use your elbows to form a cage around your face and neck. Shielding will only work for 8 to 10 seconds. But that is enough time to grab and deploy your pepper spray.

**Small items, like flashlights, pens, etc., make effective striking tools**. There are even some pepper spray units designed to be used as a kubotan or yawara stick. Hold the item inside of your fist as normal and strike with the bottom end. Use your fist as a hammer. Aim for bony, fleshy and sensitive parts such as knuckles, forearms, bridge of the nose, shins, stomach, solar plexus, spine, ribs, groin, neck and eyes. Repeat as needed.

### Elbow Strikes
Hard and pointy elbows are very effective in delivering damaging strikes. There are three main types of elbow strikes: front, back and side.

**Front elbow strikes** are delivered by swinging your elbow forward to hit targets in front of your chest. To build power, swing your shoulders and step towards the point of impact. This works even better if you grasp the fist of the striking arm with your other hand.

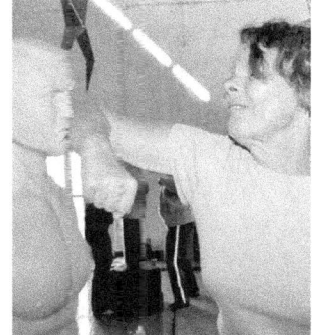

**Back elbow strikes** are delivered by swinging your elbow rearward to hit an attacker that is close behind you. To build power, swing the shoulder of your striking arm back with speed and power and step back towards the point of impact or just lift the foot on your striking side. This works even better if you grasp the fist of the striking arm with your other hand.

**Side elbow strikes** are delivered by swinging your elbow laterally from your shoulder area to hit targets directly to your side. To build power, sidestep towards the point of impact. This works even better if you grasp the fist of the striking arm with your other hand.

Elbows can deliver a devastating blow, The drawback is you need to be very close to effectively launch an elbow strike.

### Palm Strikes
Without extensive instruction, training and practice, punching an assailant is as likely to injure your hand as to stop an attacker. Bend your fingers at the second knuckle so the fingertips touch the top of your palm. Keep your thumb tight to side of your hand. Generate power from legs and hips. Target the nose, chin and/or the area around the ear and hinge of the jaw.

### Hammer Fist
If you've ever banged your fist down on a table you already know how to do a hammer strike. Strike full power with the bottom of your fist. Targets are nose, temples, and collarbones.

### Head Butts
Your forehead and the top of your head can deliver a damaging, fight-ending blow. Here's a few ways to do it:
- Forward head butts are delivered by slamming your forehead down on the attacker's face Grabbing their neck or collar and pulling them toward you amplifies the effectiveness.

- Butting with the top of the head is done by smashing the top of your head into the opponent's chin or face. This is accomplished by slightly bending your knees, then jumping upwards Against an attack from behind, by placing the back of your head against their chest and then jumping upwards.

### Defense Against Attacker On Top
If you are knocked to the ground it is likely the attacker may climb on top of you to continue their attack. Don't panic, you can use the strength of your legs to get them off of you.

1. Pull your legs in so your heels touch your rear end.
2. Shove your hips up hard as you can.
3. Twist and lift your hips forcefully.

## Safety and Self Defense Tools

**Introduction-**
A tool is defined as a device or item used to perform a task or achieve a goal.   Take time explore the different types of safety/self-defense tools available to assist you, the real estate professional, go about your business without being victimized and return home safely.   Choose the for YOUR needs.

Tools can be high tech or low tech.  Some tools are benign, presenting little likelihood of causing harm to the user or others. Other tools can cause severe, even fatal, bodily harm.  A tool may be passive, requiring little or no actions by the user or may need the user to take an action or series of actions.   There is no "one size fits all" tool perfect for everyone under all circumstances.  When selecting a tool you must consider how it will fit with your skills, abilities and personality.

This information is intended to help you make informed decisions in selecting, carrying and using safety tools. The author of this book makes no recommendation or provides any guarantee that any particular tool will protect you from danger.  You must consider which, if any of these tools, best meets your personal and professional lives.

**Apps and Alarms**
Yes, your smartphone can do wonderful things, including help keep you safe on and off the job.  At the same time, you should apply the same rules and standards you do with anything else you might put in your purse or pocket or leave on your nightstand.  Does it do what you want or need it to do? Is it safe? Is it clean?

Like many people, you may have downloaded a free flashlight app.   What a neat and handy little app!  In an emergency your phone can provide a bright, steady light in a dark stairwell, if your car has a breakdown or you dropped something in a dark place.  You know what else a flashlight app can do? Track your location, read your calendar, use your camera, install malicious applications, sell your information to marketers and spam you back to the dark ages.   Some experts claim that 75 to 80 percent of popular free apps (and nearly 100 percent of flashlight apps) on Android phones or iPhones can put your privacy at risk.

Because technology in general, and apps in particular, continues to change with extreme rapidity this book will not review specific apps or devices.  Rather, the intent is to provide you with information you can use to make good choices for your needs.

**Safety Tips for Safety Apps**
Before you download and install a safety, or any other, app to your device do your research.  Ask your friends and colleagues what they use, and how often, as well as how long they have had it.  Read reviews to learn what other users have experienced.   Find out as much as you can about the developer.  Who owns them? Where are they located?  What business are they in?

Read the permissions you're giving permission to. Be sure you understand what information the app is gathering, what files it can access and what functions it can control. For instance, why does a flashlight app need to take pictures, view your wi-fi connection or track your exact location?

It is a mistake to think every app is safe. Only downloading from Apple or Google sites will help.  Still, with over a million apps available and new ones being launched every day, Google's Play Store and Apple's App Store can't thoroughly vet every app on offer.  Think before you download an app.  If you are not one hundred percent sure, check out the app using one of the online mobile security services. Even better, use more than one.  The last thing you want for a safety app is to be less safe.

## Features and Benefits of Safety Apps

**Cost Considerations-** There's no such thing as a free app. App developers need to get paid. If you're not a paying customer then you're probably the product. That is not necessarily bad, you just need to know what you're paying to get it "free". Free apps may use up your device's memory, battery life or increase your data usage, which can wind up costing you money. Paid apps can range from just a couple of dollars to forty plus dollars per month. Some apps are included with other services such as lead tracking/management applications or security systems.

**Functionality-** In order to make a good choice of what safety app or apps will best meet your needs you'll need to know what options are available.

**Safety timers** will automatically initiate an alert if you don't cancel it by the time you specified. If you have been abducted or are restrained and can't get to your phone to cancel, your contacts and/or the police will be notified and typically provided with your (phone's) location.

**Lights and sirens** alert other nearby people that you need help. If you are unable to yell or run, a loud siren and a bright, strobing light may get you the help you need.

**A deadman's trigger** will activate an app's alert and other emergency functions in the event you are not able to. Activate the app when you feel unsafe. A panic button appears on screen, which you hold until you feel safe. Then you enter your PIN to cancel the alert. If you fail to enter the PIN after releasing the button and the PIN is not entered, the app takes action to call for help.

**Emergency Notification** functions will send an alert and your location to friends, family members and colleagues. They will also be sent your location. Some security industry experts feel that is better and safer to make people aware when you have an emergency than police or an alarm company central station. They're reasoning that the police may not place a high priority when they receive an alarm directly or transmitted from a central station. In many communities, an unverified, non-specific alarm is not considered an emergency. Depending on the jurisdiction, law enforcement responding to an alarm may not aggressively seek to clarify the nature and seriousness of an alarm call. They may be limited to knocking on the door or walking around the perimeter of the building. If they do not notice a problem they'll drive off to the next call. Family and friends are more likely to keep trying to find you regardless of the time and effort needed.

**Central Stations** also called, alarm centers, employ trained operators who can provide advice and assistance in a variety of emergencies. Some apps allow an operator to listen in live in order to furnish emergency information to responding law enforcement, when the user may be unable to.

**Location Tracking** enables you to select one or more people from your contacts list, who can then track you to your intended destination. If you have an unexpected change in your route they can contact authorities or take other actions.

**Prospect Vetting** apps let you check out clients before meeting with them. An agent alerts the potential client they want to verify them before their meeting. A text is sent to the buyer's cell phone number, who responds by answering a few simple questions and attaching a photo of a picture id.

**Keep in mind even with a perfect safety app on your device you should assume you will have to physically defend yourself from an attacker for at least two minutes, and probably much longer, until help arrives.**

**Safety Devices**

Low-cost, GPS tracking devices can be concealed in your car or on your person so you can be found in an emergency. Some of these units also will signal you need help if they detect the impact of a car crash.

Can jewelry save your life? Many companies now offer "smart" jewelry including watches, necklaces, and bracelets that connect to your mobile phone. In an emergency, a panic button function and a microphone are easier to use and less conspicuous than having to reach for your phone. Other vendors are marketing pendants and key fob devices that connect you through your cellphone in an emergency.

### Firearms

According to a February 2015 survey by the National Association of Realtors, 12 percent of responding NAR members carry a gun on the job. Evidence suggests that well-trained, responsible, law abiding, armed citizens are not only safer themselves, they make others safer as well. But carrying a gun is not the best solution for everyone.

If you're considering taking a gun with you on the job you need to know with certainty that you can make flawless "Shoot – Don't Shoot" decisions under high stress situations. The training requirements in most states are not at all adequate. Should you decide to carry a pistol, or even if you're just weighing your options, seek out an instructor who will put you in uncomfortable, high stress situations and then require you to make extremely rapid "Shoot – Don't Shoot" decisions. Repeat your training twice a year at a bare minimum.

Remember, just because you own one or more firearms for personal protection does not mean you have all the skills and decision making abilities to deal appropriately with a threat under real-life stress situations. So, if you are suddenly put in a critical situation you may either fail to respond, or may respond in a way that puts yourself or others at even higher risk. Shooting practice at a range by itself will not solve this problem. Ongoing training from a well-qualified instructor is the key.

### Gun Facts for Real Estate Agents

- Guns can only protect you if they are immediately accessible and loaded. A pistol in your car, or at the bottom of your purse will take too long to retrieve in an emergency. An average adult male can cover twenty feet of ground in less than a second from a standing start. Criminals try to strike without providing any warning, so you may have even less time.

- Warning shots are not an option. If you unholster and aim your weapon you must be ready and willing to shoot to kill.

- If you're going somewhere that you feel requires you to carry a gun for safety, you are better off choosing not to go there.

- Predators have a plan that probably includes using the element of surprise against you. It is very likely you won't even know you are being attacked until you get hit. Then you must pull, aim and discharge your weapon after receiving a blow to the head or a punch to the solar plexus. If you fail to do so with speed and accuracy there is a strong chance your attacker will take possession of your gun. Again, training is required to give you the chance to survive.

### Blunt and Edged Weapons

Blunt or impact weapons include clubs, sticks, larger flashlights, etc. Edged weapons include knives, hatchets, etc. According to one 2011 survey, conducted by Moby, a safety app developer, about 10 percent of male agents and 2.2 percent of female agents carry a knife while working. A National Association of Realtors 2015 report found that about three percent of respondents have armed themselves with a stick, baton or other blunt/impact weapon.

Blunt and impact weapons require strength and probably some skills training to be effective. Once again, a rapid decision while experiencing high levels of stress, to inflict serious or even fatal damage to another human is required. Therefore, edged and blunt weapons should not be considered a good first choice for a defense tool. Still, in an emergency situation you should use whatever self-defense tools are at hand.

**Stunguns and Tasers**
The terms stun guns and Tasers are often used interchangeably but are very different devices.

Only electroshock weapons sold by Taser International are Tasers. A "Taser" fires two small, dart-like, electrodes into a person's flesh that remain connected to the main unit by wires. One or more electric shocks are administered which disrupt the subject's control of their muscles. A civilian quality Taser costs about $300 and the cartridges for them run about $25 each. A new cartridge is needed every time the Taser is used.

"Stun gun" is the generic name for small electroshock weapons. Use of a stun gun requires that the two attack probes be directly pressed against the attacker while pressing the trigger. This will cause a moderate to severe level of pain and disrupt voluntary muscle control.

Electroshock weapons can be effective for defense and allow for self-defense against an attacker with little chance of serious bodily harm or death. But there are a number or drawbacks-

- Electroshock weapons are considered firearms in many states. Therefore, they cannot be legally carried on your person or within your reach, grasp or lunge while driving, unless you have obtained a concealed carry permit. This greatly reduces the chances you will have it handy if you need it.

- Stun guns, require you to be less than arm's length from your attacker. It is almost always better to be further away from an attacker, not closer.

- Electroshock weapons do not work through thick clothing like raincoats or leather jackets.

- Stun guns require you hold the weapon against your attacker for four or more seconds. This may prove impossible to do against an aggressive and determined foe.

- An electroshock weapon can be taken and used against you.

**Improvised Self-Defense Tools**

Since criminal attacks most often occur without any warning it is possible to find yourself in a situation which requires you to improvise a self –defense tool from available items. Most locations offer a number of objects that have the potential to be improvised self-defense tools.

- Holding your keys so they project between your fingers and then punching an assailant is recommended by many self-defense instructors. This may be effective, but only if you have proper training that allows you to hit hard, fast and accurately. In addition, you must be prepared to strike the eyes or trachea of the opponent. Anywhere else will likely result in only minor scratches or puncture wounds. These concerns also hold true regarding the use "self-defense keychains" that are built and sold for this purpose.

- Any hard object that can be grabbed in one or both hands can be used a striking tool. This includes, pens, cans of soup, candlesticks, water bottles, books, etc. Success depends on using full power from the start and striking sensitive targets like the sciatic nerve, floating ribs, brachial plexus, etc.

- Almost any type of aerosol spray can may be used for self-defense. Wasp spray, hair spray, cooking spray and spray paint all can be effective. Aim for the face, run to a safe place and get help. Some "experts" tout wasp spray or even cleaning sprays as being more effective that pepper spray for self-defense. However, there is little or no evidence to sustain this and a number of online videos of people being sprayed with these show them as being less than effective.

- Fire extinguishers can be effective for self-defense and are quite ubiquitous. Spray the attacker and them hit them with it before fleeing to a safe location and calling 911.

- Ordinary credit cards can be used to slice a predator's forehead. This will create a significant flow of blood into their eyes, providing an opportunity to escape and get help.

- Any granular substance such as sand, salt or sugar can be flung into the eyes of an assailant. Even if they are wearing glasses, enough should get into their eyes to cause discomfort and reduced vision, so you can find a secure location and safely call for help.

- Any hard object that can be thrown may work as a self-defense tool. The object should be heavy enough to hit with effective force.

## Self-Defense Spray

A National Association of Realtors 2015 report found that 17 percent of responding Realtors carry self-defense spray. For most people, whether or not they're employed in the real estate field, self-defense spray is the best choice. Many people, (including news reporters) call all self-defense sprays MACE. However, MACE is a trademarked product and its original formula is no longer available although the company continues to sell one mixed with pepper spray and other products.

MACE, CS, CN and tear gas are chemical irritants. These manmade chemicals cause pain to the eyes, nose, throat, and lung tissues. Significant production of tears and mucus also occurs. A major shortcoming of all these irritant products is that they are not effective on people who have a high pain tolerance because they are drunk, agitated, high on drugs, mentally ill or just have a high pain threshold. Even worse, a certain percentage of the population responds to pain by becoming even angrier and experiences a strong adrenaline fueled reaction. The result is a madder, stronger attacker, just the opposite of the intended effect. They also do not have much effect on animals.

In contrast, pepper spray is an inflammatory agent. It will cause an attacker's eyes to swell shut. There have been reports of some people holding their eyes open with their fingers, but their hand cannot be used to continue an attack. This temporary loss of vision often causes fear and disorientation. Swelling of mucus membranes in the nose and bronchial passages, usually accompanied by spasmodic coughing, reduce the subject's ability to breathe in enough oxygen to continue an attack.

Pepper spray is also known as oleoresin capsicum, OC or capsicum spray when it is intended for use on humans. When it is intended for stopping bears and dog attacks it is called bear spray or HALT respectively. Popular brands include VEXOR, Sabre, MACE, Bodyguard, Streetwise and Fox Labs.

The active ingredient in pepper spray is capsicum, which is a chemical distilled from the same the hot peppers you may enjoy eating. Hot and sweet peppers are part of them, which includes the mild, inoffensive bell peppers, chili peppers, jalapenos, habaneros, cayenne and many more. It is estimated 50,000 capsicum varieties are grown around the world. The "hotness" of peppers is rated in Scoville Heat Units or SHUs. If you have rubbed your eyes after handling a jalapeno pepper, you experienced about 2500 SHUs. Pepper sprays currently are being sold with SHU ratings of between 500,000 and 15 million.

There is no single self defense method that is 100% reliable and 100% risk free, but pepper spray does come close. One study (The Effectiveness and Safety of Pepper Spray, Office of Justice Programs, National Institute of Justice), found OC spray successfully incapacitated humans in 156 out of 174 (90 percent) confrontations when deployed by police. Even when a person is not completely incapacitated by a dose of OC their ability to commit violence will be downgraded. A 1999 study of 690 incidents of pepper spray use by law enforcement found pepper spray was effective 85 percent of the time, according to the broadest definition of the term "effectiveness."

Keychain units, that hold a half-ounce of liquid OC, are generally the best choice to carry on a regular basis. There are several manufacturers who use the same hard-shell ½ ounce case, so you cannot judge a pepper spray by its looks. Read the label and do your research. Most, if not all of hard-shell, ½ ounce units include a built-in belt clip.

Pepper spray canisters that hold two or more ounces are good choices for your home, business or vehicle and for those who plan on keeping it in a holster.

Pepper sprays disguised as pens or lipsticks have the advantage of being able to hide in plain sight. However, the three steps of removing the cap, aiming and then pushing the top down to fire make them slower to use in ambush type situations. Also, you will need to look at it, instead of at the assailant, to be sure you're aiming correctly. While these are not recommended for regular carrying situations they may be a good choice if you anticipate being a victim of domestic or acquaintance violence.

Pepper sprays that come in soft, leatherette holsters with snap shut top straps are not recommended as it takes too long to unsnap the top, turn the trigger, aim and fire. It is also very likely that the holster's top strap will flop around and interfere with the spray.

**Pepper Spray Legal Considerations:** Pepper spray is legal in all fifty states, but laws do vary. Check state and local laws before carrying pepper spray. Never use your pepper spray for any reason except to protect yourself or others from physical harm, sexual assault or abduction! Using pepper spray because someone has been rude, insulting, driving poorly or any reason other than a clear and immediate threat may result in your arrest.

### Using Your OC Spray

**Ready!** Keep your pepper spray in your pocket, clipped to your belt or where it can be easily found in your purse whenever you are in any type of risky situation. and quickly reached with your dominant hand. Whenever you sense a potential threat position your hand on your spray ready to fire. REMEMBER TO SWITCH THE OC SPRAY'S TRIGGER BACK TO "SAFE" IF MOVED TO THE "FIRE"POSITION!

Stand "bladed" by turning sideways to the aggressor. Your dominant hand holds the OC (find **ON** trigger ready to shoot), and is extended out about ¾ of a full extension. Position your non-dominant, rearward hand, about ½ way between your head and the dominant, forward, shoulder. Keep the rear hand open. Its job is to protect your face and throat. Your feet are slightly wider than your shoulders. Attempt to keep as much distance between you as practical.

**AIM!** The aiming point for pepper spray is the center of the face. Most pepper sprays have an effective range of six to ten feet, but read the instruction that came in the package and perform a test fire to be sure.

**FIRE!** Maximum results are obtained when the assailant's eyes are swollen shut due to the inflammatory effect of the spray and the bronchial passages are inflamed enough to cause spasmodic coughing. Spraying an attacker on the chest, hands, etc. will not be effective in stopping an attack. Some people are able to withstand the pain and continue to function. However, the temporary blindness caused by the direct application of OC to the eyes greatly reduces their ability to find their victim and launch an effective attack. When pepper spray droplets contact the bronchial passages the intense coughing makes it very difficult to breath in enough air to maintain a sustained physical attack. In addition, the involuntary, spasmodic coughing reduces their ability to concentrate and focus.

When driving you may decide to carry a pepper spray for protection. Use either a keychain unit attached to your key ring or a canister in the center console or other easy to reach location. In order to avoid ever needing your spray practice the following safe driving techniques—

1. Always lock your doors and start the car immediately upon entering. Fasten your seat belt, put your phone in its holder, look at your receipts, and buckle in the kids only AFTER the doors are secured and the motor is started.

2. In traffic or at a stoplight, leave enough space between your car and the one in front so you can maneuver and drive away.

3. Road rage is a dangerous and stupid response to certain, rude, aggressive or dangerous behaviors another driver engages in. These behaviors stimulate a primitive part of the human mind, known as the " reptilian brain". Road-rage happens when the reptilian mind feels threatened and responds aggressively as it feels its/your survival is on the line. The rational parts of the mind are no longer in

control and a minor incident now turns into a violent encounter. Road rage can be prevented or mitigated by:
- Keeping control of your own temper.
- Not reacting to another driver's bad behavior.
- Practicing good, courteous driving habits.

If you find yourself being threatened by an aggressive driver, ignore verbal abuse and rude gestures. Do not engage the aggressor. Keep your doors locked and your windows up. Do not stop or get out of the car. If you are being followed, call 911, head to the nearest police station or any other public place where there is help.

If you try to use pepper spray through the window of a stopped or moving vehicle it may blow back into your face. The only time to use pepper spray inside a vehicle is if the attacker is also in the car.

### Pepper Spray vs. Armed Attackers
Should you use your OC spray when the attacker has a weapon? If the assailant only wants your property, money, jewelry, car, etc. then give it up and don't fight. If they want to relocate you, put you in a vehicle, or restrain you in anyway, you must take action, as your chances of survival plummet. Perpetrators are not tying you up for your benefit. They are not taking you to someplace where it will be easier to escape. Your best chance of surviving is to take action now.

Running away, if possible, is recommended, as it is almost always the best choice. Keep in mind the police hit their targets only one time out of five in actual confrontations. No doubt, the chances that a criminal will hit you are even less. And there's even a smaller chance you'll be hit in a vital area. Of course, all else being equal, wouldn't you rather be shot in a public space than in an empty field somewhere?

In this situation you'll need to stay calm and avoid any sudden moves. A quick grab for your pepper spray may make the attacker think you're reaching for a gun, causing them to shoot you. Should you decide to spray the attacker, do it fast and immediately run away. If you're in a confined location, move away quietly making it harder to locate and aim for you.

### First Aid for Pepper Spray
Should you accidentally spray yourself or another person the recommended first aid is to flush the affected area with cold water. Rinse out the mouth and suck on an ice cube or chips. If the exposure occurred indoors going outside for fresh air may help restore normal breathing. If symptoms persist for more than a few minutes after first aid has been administered contact your local Poison Control Center.

### Is Wasp Spray Better Than Pepper Spray
Many people believe carrying wasp spray for self-defense is a good idea. However, the evidence that wasp spray is effective at stopping violent attacks is minimal at best. In fact, there's no research that wasp spray would stop an attacker. There can be legal issues, as using an insecticide in manner different than use listed on the label is a violation of Federal law. You are not likely to be arrest, but you could face a lawsuit from your assailant. Your liability is likely to be significant if you intentionally spray a person with a pesticide. Wasp spray has not been tested on humans, so the only human toxicity data is a result of accidental exposures and suicide attempts. There are several videos online that show people being sprayed with bug spray with very little effect. Nevertheless, in an emergency situation use whatever you have available.

## Frauds, Scams, Financial Crimes and Identify Theft

Robbing people with guns is a high-risk, low-payoff crime. Smarter criminals stick to financial and online crime because they are low-risk and can pay big. Hackers and swindlers may get arrested, but they rarely get shot. Some examples financial and techno-crime include:

- Hackers siphoned off "between $100,000 and $200,000" sent by Maryland homebuyers to what they believed was the correct bank for their home purchase.

- A Boston property management firm was fined $15,000 after the theft of a company laptop containing the personal information of over 600 residents.

- Hackers stole $80,000 in closing funds and $20,000 in earnest-money deposits by penetrating a Massachusetts buyer's agent's email account and supplying false bank wiring instructions.

- Settlement funds cams are affecting "hundreds if not thousands" of home closings causing the Federal Trade Commission and the National Association of Realtors to issue a warning about the threats.

- A Miami real estate agent and married mother of two, reported that she was receiving hundreds of unsolicited phone calls and text messages from strangers inquiring about sex. Callers found her number in an escort ad at Craigslist.org, posted by another local agent who was upset after she closed a transaction that cost him a commission.

### Money Laundering in Residential Real Estate

In residential real estate, money laundering occurs when criminal proceeds are used to purchase property. When money is obtained from illegal activities, or is being hidden from tax authorities, it needs to be "laundered" through the financial system, so its original source is disguised.

In one common method the seller understates the value of the property in official documents. The buyer/launderer makes up the difference by paying with cash obtained through criminal proceeds. The buyer later sells the property for a higher price, and pockets the profits. Now, it appears the money was earned through legitimate means.

A more sophisticated technique for money laundering may also involve buying property, with money illegally obtained and transferred through a number of shell companies so that its origins are difficult to determine. When this property is sold, it seems like a legitimate transaction.

Another way to launder money is to have a relative "gift' money to help get a mortgage. The relative is then reimbursed in unreported cash.

Indicators of possible money laundering can be detected by vigilant real estate agents, based on their knowledge of the real estate industry and how transactions are normally conducted. It's important to look at the whole picture when trying to determine if money laundering is present and whether or not you should request more information or seek additional help. Indicators of potential money laundering include:

Money is transferred from a country that has an unstable government, or is known for high levels of corruption. If you suspect funds are coming from country of origin fits one or more of these categories, check with the Office of Foreign Assets Control (OFAC).

Titling a residential property in the name of a third party, such as a shell corporation, may be an effort to hide the identity of the real owner. Shell corporations are legally formed, but are used to hide ownership from the public or the government.

If the buyer seems uninterested in bargaining for a price reduction or if property is being sold for significantly less than market value.

- Large amounts of cash are used to make the transaction.

- The buyer does not seek a mortgage to pay for the property.

- A buyer's occupation or income does not square with the type of property.

- Very fast resale of the property with a resale price is dramatically higher or lower without explanation.

- The buyer is demanding a very fast transaction, in particular if the buyer does not want to view the property.

Real estate professionals can help identify and combat money laundering. Knowing your customer, their interest in, and planned use for a property will help you evaluate a situation when one or more red flags are present.

The requirement that a real estate agent develops a reasonable belief that the true identity of a customer is known is referred to as know-your-customer or customer due diligence. You can then be able to determine the likelihood that money laundering is being committed. In cases where red flags are present, be prepared to apply increased levels of due diligence, which may include the following:

1. Ask for a driver's license, passport or other reliable identification document, to confirm the true identity of the customer.

2. If a corporation or LLC is involved, take additional measures to determine who really controls or owns the company.

3. Use your own experience and knowledge to understand the customer's circumstances and business. Get additional information if something doesn't seem right.

If you suspect money laundering you have the option of reporting the information to local law enforcement or the FBI. In addition, consider filing a suspicious activity report with the U.S. Treasury's Financial Crimes Enforcement Network. Suspicious activity reports are primarily intended for use by financial institutions and are important for enforcement agencies engaged in combating money laundering. Real estate professionals are not required to file a suspicious activity report, but be aware of this option if you have reasonable suspicion that a transaction may be a vehicle for illegal financing activity. Banks enjoy some immunity from civil actions when filing a suspicious activity report, but real estate professionals may not be. Therefore consulting with an attorney is a prudent step before filing a report.

**IRS Form 8300**
Form 8300 is an information report that is required to be filed by any trade or business, including banks, car dealers, etc., that receives in excess of $10,000 in cash in a single transaction or by multiple related transactions. Therefore, if for any reason a real estate agent or broker receives more than $10,000 in cash from a buyer or seller in the course of a real estate transaction, the form must be filled out and filed. Form 8300 can be obtained online or at a local IRS office.

Cash, for purposes of IRS Form 8300, also means cash equivalents such as cashier's checks, bank drafts, money orders. If the cash equivalent instrument is for more than $10,000, the transaction will be reported by the issuing bank, and the agent does not need to also file a Form 8300. If, however, an agent receives a cashier's check or other cash equivalent of less than $10,000, but which in combination with other cash or cash equivalents totals more than $10,000, a Form 8300 must be filed.

<u>**Real Risks in the Virtual World**</u>

**Hackers, Stalkers and Malware**

If you were a kid before the Internet, and lived in a big city, chances are your parents warned you never to go to a certain part of town. In Boston, it was "The Combat Zone", Chicago had South State Street and San Francisco had the Tenderloin. These locations were famous for pornography, prostitution, street crimes and violence. Most of these pockets of vice have been cleaned up or maybe just put out of business by the Internet. The Internet is like having a high crime hot spot in your office, home or pocket. And while you may not be interested in the darker parts of the Internet, the darker parts are interested in you.

Not long ago the worst possible harm from online crimes was limited to corrupting your files. Back then the only device connected to the information superhighway was your computer. Now buying, banking and business are commonplace and the once clear lines between the virtual and the real world are being increasingly blurred. The emergence of "the Internet of Things" by tying our computers, appliances, HVAC systems, cars, security systems and door locks to our smartphones and devices promises great benefits. It also unlocks our money, privacy and physical security. Telephones have morphed into networked data devices that look and act like phones. Late model cars have become networked transportation devices. The network is everywhere and in almost everything.

Criminals have always been quick to take advantage of new technology, and social changes. Whenever the next big thing comes along criminals quickly adopt and exploit them. When railroads expanded, robbers realized it was safer and easier for them to rob a train in an isolated location than to rob a well-protected bank in a populated area. So, most types of tech crimes are just plain old crime adapted from the real world for use online. There were con men, scammers, burglars, etc. before there were computers but now they can strike without even leaving the comfort of their parent's basement.

There are many different kinds of cyber crime and new ones emerging all the time. Examples of cyber crime include: data theft, digital vandalism, fraud, scams, identity theft, harassment, malware, ransomware and spyware. Chances are you have already been victimized at least once. And it is a virtual certainty you are being targeted right now. You cannot eliminate all risks from cyber crime. But, you can choose to take precautions and make preparations to reduce your odds of being a victim and mitigating damage when it happens.

**Keyloggers -** It has often been said, "You are what you eat." Today, "You are what you type on your keyboard." A keylogger is an application, running in the background, logging every keystroke you make. They grab and store data like credit card numbers, passwords, etc. before sending off to who knows who. Parents, or employers can legitimately use keyloggers, but they are also used by those who do not have your best interests at heart. There are two main types of keyloggers:

- Hardware-based keyloggers do not require software be installed but do require physical access to the computer or other device to be installed. Because they are not running on the devices operation system they are often missed by malware detection software. These can be small USB sticks, inline with the keyboard's cable connector or in some cases built into the keyboard itself.
- Software-based keyloggers must be installed on a computer where they then capture, save and share whatever you type. Software-based keyloggers may or may not be more detectable by security applications. Keyloggers infect devices in the same way that other malicious programs spread. Keyloggers can be installed on your system when you open a file attachment received via email, text message, P2P networks, instant message or social networks. One very common method is to send an email from what appears to be a trusted source but is in fact either is coming from a contact who has been hacked or by using an email address that resembles a legitimate one, for example Pat@abc.jpn instead of Pat@abc.com. Keyloggers can also be installed just by visiting a website if that site is infected.

Completely protecting your data from keyloggers is close to impossible. Because they are small, and use very little bandwidth when transmitting what was keyed in, there is not a noticeable reduction in a computer's performance.

## **Password Security**

Have you ever been a victim of a hacker or had your identity stolen? Chances are good that you have and chances are just as good you were an accomplice. An unwitting and unwilling accomplice, but an accomplice all the same. No, you did not deserve to be a victim any more than leaving a door unlocked means you deserve to burglarized. Behaviors that increase your risk or cyber crime include:

- Re-using passwords
- Using weak passwords
- Installing a keylogger (No, you didn't mean to when you clicked on that PDF attachment, but you still did.)
- Posting answers to security questions on social media
- Failing to install, update and use anti-malware applications on all your devices

Sophisticated hacker groups can use massive processing power in a brute force attack to crack your passwords. But most of the time they don't need to because targets, like you, make it so easy to guess. The Mel Brooks movie, "Spaceballs" contained a running joke about using "12345" as a password and how only an idiot would use it. Since the movie's debut in 1987 it seems nothing has changed. The most common passwords today are 123456, password, 123456password, 12345678, qwerty, 12345 Password, and 12345678qwerty. Do you see one of your passwords here?

Okay, you're too security smart to use a password that was a joke in a 30 year old movie. Your passwords are unique, creative and really hard to guess. Or are they? Human behavior is rather predictable. We really do tend to think and act alike more than we are comfortable admitting. When creating a new password we are likely to have similar thought processes. Your kids' and pets' names, favorite movie, or sports team make lousy passwords. The best passwords use long combinations of letters, numbers and other characters. Common words, phrases, short strings of numbers are extremely risky. To create strong passwords:

- Use a mix of numbers, letters and symbols.
- Eight characters is the bare minimum, but the longer the better
- Passwords are case sensitive, so mix up cases, for example: sUpermAn.
- Swap numbers and symbols for letters, like - M0N3Y instead if money, with a zero replacing an "o" and 3 for an "e". Spaces aren't always allowed so it is best to avoid them.
- Use two-factor authentication requiring both a password AND a one-time use PIN sent to your phone, when available.

Common password creation mistakes people make include using:

- Your name or variations of your name, including backwards, initials and nicknames
- Phone numbers, social security numbers, birthdays, anniversaries and address numbers, even in reverse order
- Parts of names or IDs
- Any common name, e.g., Sue, Joe
- Passwords of fewer than eight characters
- Names of your kids and other relatives, friends, or pets
- Single words either preceded or followed by a digit, a punctuation mark, up arrow, or space.
- Well known slogans, song lyrics and phrase with spaces removed - "Where's the beef?"
- Words that can be found in a dictionary, forward, backwards, or pluralized

Taking effective password security precautions cannot stop all cyber-intrusions. But you can screen out the less sophisticated attempts and slow down more capable crooks.

**Reusing Passwords is Risky** - Now you know how to make strong passwords that will slow down anyone trying to sneak in to one of your accounts or applications. You may think this is such a great password you want to use it for all of your login credentials. Think again. Yes, it is easier to re-use your password for all your accounts and devices. And it is also easier to compromise your security when you do. If your login is compromised then all of your accounts are now placed at risk.

Recycle paper, plastic and soda cans, but not your passwords. Reusing passwords across different accounts represents a risk. All a hacker needs to do is to crack one site to gain the keys to the kingdom. If a trusted account suffers a data breach your password can be exposed. Or, if scammers set up a bogus web page that offers you a free eBook of the best real estate success tips ever. All you need to do is enter your email and set up a password. The scammer may or may not send that eBook, but if you are recycling passwords they can try the one you just entered and see where it gets them. If you entered your email password then basically you're naked on the Internet. Many websites require or encourage users to log in using their e-mail, LinkedIn, Facebook or email accounts which has the effect of multiplying your risk.

<u>**How to Spot a Scam Webpage**</u>
Scams often depend on victims not knowing how the DNS naming structure for domains works. Look at the last part of a domain name, the domain name <u>info</u>.example.com would be a child domain of example.com because example.com appears at the end of the full domain name (on the right-hand side). But, example.maliciousscammers.com is not really from example.com because the name "example" is on the left side of the domain name. Look for signs such as:
- Mismatched URL
- Misleading domain name
- Poor spelling and grammar

<u>**Email Security**</u>
The first email ever was sent in 1971 by computer engineer Ray Tomlinson to himself and consisted of nonsense letters like "qwertyuiop". When the first scam email was sent is not know, but "spam" has been around since at least 1978 and "Phishing" since 1981 or longer. The first computer virus to be distributed in "the wild" was called "brain" and created by two brothers, Basit and Amjad Farooq Alvi, in an attempt to stop customers from making unauthorized copies of the software they were selling on floppy disks. Spam, phishing, viruses and frauds have been popping up in inboxes ever since.

The most common email scams, called 'advance fee scams" have been in use for hundreds of years before email was invented. The techniques are the same, the technology has changed. A prince, government official, or banker has an enormous fortune, but in order to get it they need your help. The message has enough details about a current event that is seems plausible, at least at first glance. All you need to do is wire them a small amount of money (the advance fee), so they can pay a bribe, custom fees, bail or the like. If you take the bait and wire the cash, it will never go smoothly. Never! There's a new government official, the bail bond was increased, or one more lawyer is needed. You'll be strung along in an attempt to keep your wire transfers coming until you wise up or go broke.

Amazingly, these scams are still effective, bilking billions from businesses. According to the FBI:

- Law enforcement globally has received complaints from every U.S. state and in at least 79 countries.
- From October 2013 through February 2016, law enforcement received reports from 17,642 victims.
- This amounted to more than $2.3 billion in losses.
- Since January 2015, the FBI has seen a 270 percent increase in identified victims and exposed loss.

- In Arizona the average loss per scam is between $25,000 and $75,000.

You can refuse to become a statistic. Here is some email safety tips,

- Don't send sensitive information via unencrypted email. If you must email sensitive information, use encrypted email. Use encryption features built into your email service, or commercial encryption software or use a free application like OpenPGP.
- Never wire money until you have verified the wiring instructions with the intended recipient. Verify the telephone number you're calling to confirm with.
- Do not trust contact information in an unverified email. Fraudulent emails often have legitimate-looking signature blocks with untraceable telephone numbers and links to fake websites. Going directly to the company's website by browser and using a reverse telephone directory to double-check a phone number takes seconds but can save you from making a bad mistake.
- Never click on any links in an unverified email. In addition to leading you to fake websites, these links can contain viruses and other malicious spyware that can make your computer, and your transactions vulnerable to attack.
- Don't do sensitive business over unsecured, public, wifi, especially if it's something very sensitive like banking or credit card info. Wait until you get home or to the office.
- Warn clients that if an email or a telephone call ever seems suspicious in any way, they should refrain from taking any action until they check with you.
- Delete sensitive emails as quick as you can. If it has something you'll need going forward, save in a more secure location.
- Change your login info on a regular basis schedule.
- Keep firewall and anti-virus technologies up to date.

The weakest link in your cyber-security is not located out on the Internet in cyberspace but is between your ears in cranial space.

**Phishing and Spear Phishing**
A phishing attack attempts to acquire usernames, passwords, credit card and other information by posing as a well-known business or government entity. These emails try to look realistic and authentic but often, not always, contain typos, grammatical errors and other mistakes upon closer examination. Phishing attempts are blasted out to an enormous number of email addresses. The fraudster is relying on enough people falling for the scam to make a profit.

One well known example involved emails purported to be from The Post Office, FedEx, United Parcel Service or other delivery companies, directing reader to print an attached label in pdf, doc or safe looking file format extension. But clicking on the attachment loads malware on to your computer. This scam and a new version of it pops up between Thanksgiving and Christmas when people send and receive a lot of packages, tend to be hectic and so may be more likely to drop their guard.

Spear phishing is crafted to target a specific individual or group and contains detailed information to make it appear to be bona fide. Using information you put on the Internet, including social networking sites, your webpage, email addresses your friends left un-redacted on those endlessly FWD'ed emails, new stories and even legitimate data brokers. A spear phisher may pose as a friend, colleague or vendor to send you an email in hopes you'll accept it as real. It may ask you to send a password, arrange a transfer of funds or just get you to click on a link that will install malware on your device. Spear phishing attempts will often include an urgent call to action such as, "Failure to respond will result in your account being frozen," or "Avoid additional fines and penalties by responding promptly," hoping to create enough panic that you'll respond before taking time to think.

Florida Realtor Tania Harmon posted this spear phishing story on her blog. *"REALTORS, SELLERS, BUYERS BEWARE! Yesterday after a morning closing the title company received an email supposedly from me asking the closing funds be wired to a different account other than to the seller's bank account.*

*They even provided a signed document from two of the sellers giving permission to do so. Luckily there were 3 sellers on title so the title company called me to confirm and asked for a permission slip from the third seller. When I told her that I had not requested this to be done we discovered that it was a fraud and the money was sent to the proper sellers account. Immediately I changed my email password and spent two hours with my email provider making sure my account was cleaned out. We tried to contact the authorities to expose this fraud and we were told that nothing could be done unless the money had been transferred to the person committing the fraud. And if they were not in the US then it could not be traced. Notify your title company's to be aware of this fraud."*

*Legitimate companies and government entities don't ask for credit card and bank account numbers, Social Security numbers, passwords, etc. by email or text. Delete email and text messages that ask you to confirm or provide personal information. If you have any doubts call the company in question on the number printed on your financial statements or back of your credit card, or log on to your account directly from your browser."*

Phishers will try to direct you to spoof sites that look real but really just want to steal your information so your name and accounts can be exploited. Never reply, click on links or call phone numbers provided in the message.

**If you think you may have been hooked or speared by a phishing fraud:**

- Don't wait! Take immediate action to reduce your exposure.
- Immediately change all usernames and passwords on all your accounts.
- File a report with the FBI or local police.
- File a Federal Trade Commission report at www.ftc.gov/complaint.
- Carefully check all credit card and bank statements for suspicious activity.
- Initiate a fraud alert with any of the three major credit bureaus. The other two will also put a fraud alert on your record. Then, if someone tries to open a new account in your name, the credit grantor will call you before approving the new line of credit.
- Report any fraudulent activity to your REALTOR® association so that they can send warn others.

**<u>Preventing Identity Theft</u>**

Protecting sensitive information on and offline well help prevent identify theft. Keep your financial documents and personal records securely locked in a safe place. Secure your wallet and purse in a safe place at work and while out and about. Make extra sure to secure your information when you have contractors, carpet cleaners, or other workers at your home and office. Shred or burn unneeded documents at least twice a year.

Keep cards you rarely need locked up. Keep only the identification, credit, and debit cards you really need with you and know what you are carrying. Leave your Social Security card at home.

Before you share information at your workplace, a business, your child's school, or a doctor's office, ask why they need it, how they will safeguard it, and if it is really needed.

Shred receipts, credit offers, credit applications, insurance forms, physician statements, checks, bank statements, expired charge cards, and similar documents when you don't need them any longer.

Remove labels on prescription medications before you throw them out. Never share information about your health plan with anyone who offers unsolicited free health services or products.

Don't mail checks or documents with sensitive information from curbside or other unsecured mailboxes. Fraud artists can still info or "wash" a check then change the payee. Mail from the post office or a Secure postal collection box.

Review monthly financial statements carefully for fraudulent activity.

Ask for a free copy of your credit report from a credit-reporting agency once a year to examine it for fraudulent activity.

**BONUS TIP:** Place and renew a fraud alert on your credit file. When you place a 90 Day Fraud Alert on your credit file at any one of the three nationwide credit reporting agencies they will also notify the other two. A fraud alert requires creditors accessing your credit report to take additional precautions when handling requests to open or make changes to a credit account in your name. Both the 90 day and seven year fraud alerts are free, but to get the extended seven year alert you must provide a law enforcement report documenting that you are a victim of identity theft or mail theft.

**Mitigating Identity Theft**
If you're the victim of identity theft make sure you know your rights. In most states you're not responsible for any debt incurred on fraudulent new accounts opened in your name without your permission. Federal law limits the amount you have to pay for any and all unauthorized use of your credit card to $50. If you report the loss to the credit card company before your credit card is used by a thief, then you aren't responsible for any of the unauthorized charges.

The rules for lost or stolen ATM or debit cards are different than for credit cards. Your liability is determined by how fast you report the loss to the issuing institution. Notify them before any unauthorized charges are made and your liability is zero. Notify them within 2 business days after you learn about the loss or theft and your loss is limited to just $50. If you take more than 2 business days after you learn about the loss or theft, but less than 60 calendar days from getting your statement you're on the hook for up to $500. And if you wait more than 60 days to alert the issuer there is no limit to what you may have to pay.

If a criminal makes unauthorized debits to your bank or credit union account using your debit card number, but not your card, you aren't responsible – provided you report the problem within 60 days after receiving your account statement which shows the unauthorized debits. Most states limit your liability for fraudulent checks issued on your bank or credit union account if you notify the bank or credit union promptly. Check with your state and local consumer protection offices to learn the laws in your area.

**Social Media**
Facebook, Google+, Twitter, Instagram, LinkedIn and other social media have expanded the ways real estate professionals find and keep in touch with potential and current customers. Social media offers an opportunity to connect with your loyal clients. Social media provides an effective way to build your circle of influence by making connections with the friends of your customers' friends. Because the power of social media can be abused you need to know the risks and how to protect yourself from the anti-social side of social media.

**Social Media Hazards**
What you post about on social media can inform people with criminal intentions about your interests, lifestyle and activities. Spear-phishers like to use this information to craft messages you'll be inclined to open and click on the links inside. Stalkers can track your whereabouts. Burglars can learn when your home or office will be empty and for how long. Behaviors that increase your risks include:

- Having a lot of friends or followers on social media that you do not really know boosts your risk level.
- Accepting a friend request from a stranger.
- Over-sharing personably identifiable information.
- Posting pics with location information.

- Not using privacy settings.

**Safer Social Media Practices**
- Grow your social networks slowly, value quality or quantify. Cyber-criminals can exploit your name and reputation exploiting your "friendship" to gain access to your friends and acquaintances. For example, if someone you know from a real world networking group gets a friend request from a stranger, they'll be more likely to accept if they notice that you are also are connected to the requester. Each time a cyber criminal connects with a member of your network, they gain credibility. Like ripples on a pond, they send friend requests to all of your friends and their friends' friends, to gain trust and harvest details about potential victims.

- Take the time to question every single friend request. Accept those you know in real life. If you've never seen their name before, either ignore the request or send a message asking who they are and why they want to be your "friend." Scammers know social media users are more likely to accept a friend request from strangers with photos and a long list of contacts on the social media accounts. People are also more likely to approve a friend request from someone that lists well known, high status connections. Requests from attractive females are more likely to be okayed by both men and women.

- Use the built in privacy management tools and check them on a regular schedule. On Facebook for instance, find the padlock icon on the top-bar, and click it to bring down the "Privacy Shortcuts" menu. The, "Who can see my stuff?" option sets limits on who can see your activities and content in the future. You can select "Friends", "Friends of Friends", or "Public". You can set limits on who can contact you and even block people from contacting you. Be sure to limit your Timeline and/or past posts to friends only.

- Third-party applications require extra scrutiny. Applications that seem suspicious should be avoided. Be sure you understand what information you're allowing the app access to before installing.

- Disable auto login on any device you do not always keep securely in your control.

- Never post your sensitive information including:
- Complete and true birth date
- Location information
- Home phone number
- Social Security Number, not even just the last four digits
- Pictures of your kids with their names
- Vacation plans
- Anything you wouldn't want your employer, customers or family to see
- Photos that show your location either visible or imbedded in meta data

- Always log off any public or shared computer and use the "Incognito" or "Private Window" browser mode.

- Buy, use and update anti-virus software that blocks, detects and removes malware to help keep your identity safe.

To stay safe, think of social media platforms as online bus stations. Choose what image you want to project, what information you're comfortable sharing and whom you let approach and converse with you as though you're waiting for the Greyhound.

### Photograph Hazards
Before posting pictures in online listings or on your favorite social media site you should understand some of the hidden risks. Digital cameras can help even the most inept photographers produce near professional photos. But they also can reveal your location and other information to stalkers and other criminals.

### EXIF Metadata
Most high-end models of digital cameras and all smartphones have built-in GPS units. So your smartphone probably knows exactly where you are when you take a picture, whether you are indoors or outdoors. Many devices put that information into the metadata (Called EXIF which stands for exchangeable image file format.) of every picture you take. When your photos include metadata, anyone can decode it and see if the picture was taken at your home, your office, your favorite coffee shop, at your kid's school or where ever. Most devices provide two ways to prevent your location from being attached to your photos. You can either turn off the built-in GPS unit entirely, or turn off the GPS function only for the camera, but keep it on for other functions such as driving directions.

What about picture you already took or a picture taken by others. Don't worry, it is pretty easy check to your existing photos contain location metadata. Open a picture file on your computer. By default you'll see only the picture. To find the metadata, right-click the file, click Properties, click the "Details' tab. Scroll down and look for a "GPS" section. If it's there, you'll see the photo's latitude and longitude. To clear this information just click the "Remove Properties and Personal Information."

### Reverse Image Searches
Reverse image searches check the Internet for other instances where that image was used online. Just upload an image or paste a link to a picture and you can find a photo's origin, date, the name of a product, names, or see if anyone else is using your pictures. Even when it is not the exact same picture, the "Visually Similar" features will find other photos of the same person. Use caution to keep your private and personal information from being accessed by a stalker using your business related pictures.

### Online Reputation Hazards
Before going out to dinner, seeing a movie or even trying a new dry cleaners we love to jump online and read the reviews. Buying a house or buying a pizza, people rely on Yelp and Angie's List. A majority of customers say they trust online reviews just as much as personal recommendations. If the world were a fair place we would all be able to rely on reviews as gospel and the reviewers as fair, impartial and reasonable. But the world is not a fair place. Consumers are more likely to post a review after a negative experience than a positive one. Worse still, an angry person with a grievance can destroy a good reputation that took you years of hard work to build. If you make your living in real estate your reputation is your single most important asset. You need to grow, watch it and protect it.

Avoid online reputation disasters, and minimize them if they happen with the "3 M's" of reputation management.
- Monitor News and Reviews
- Master Your Domain
- Make Finding You EASY

### Monitor
If there is a problem time is not on your side. Google your name and your brokerage's name regularly. Check both the Google "all" results and news. Set up a Google alert on your name to keep track of any new content that is posted. Have notifications mailed to you once a day, so as not to overwhelm your inbox. Perform reverse image searches of your pictures to see if anyone is making unauthorized use of them.

Yelp! is one of the most important consumer review sites. In addition to dominating the review space, Yelp! content is used by many other sites and can be a major driver of Google search results. So make sure you know what is being Yelped about you. Check your reviews on Trulia, Zillow and other real estate specific sites, too.

### Manage
- Lock your domain name. Locking down your domain helps prevent unauthorized third parties from redirecting your traffic to another site.
- Record the proper domain ownership. You should be listed as the registrant or administrative contact for your domain. Check it with a WHOIS lookup to be sure it's you. The registrant or administrative contact is the actual owner of the domain. Allowing your web host to be listed as the owner can affect your options for changing contact and ownership information, renewals and moving to other service providers.
- Consider hiring a social media manager or social media management firm. Or use a social media management dashboard app to make it easier for you.

### Make Finding You EASY
- Buy variations of your domain name. The low cost of web domains makes it easy for scammers or grudge-holders to cyber-squat using a variation of your domain name or company name. Most registration services are automated and as long as the exact name is not already recorded almost any domain name gets approved.
- Buy the common versions of your domain (examples: .tv, .net, and .biz) too for the same reasons.
- Create online profiles on the most important social media and third party review sites so that someone else can't beat you to the punch. Check and update these regularly as comment trolls can abuse zombie profiles. Choose the sites that have the most impact by searching for terms like: "homes for sale with the appropriate zip code."

### If a Reputation Disaster Happens -

Social media gives you the opportunity to quickly respond to negative reviews, online rumors and negative news stories. If your real estate firm is aware a potential PR disaster is about to occur, such as an associate getting arrested, or that you're being sued, take a proactive response and break the news, telling your side of the story so that you control narrative.

- **Defuse the situation quickly before it escalates.** If a person has been wronged, often they just want to be heard and acknowledged. If a commenter is posting inaccurate information, approach them and ask if they can retract or modify their statement. If a mistake has been made by you, or one of your team, then this should also be addressed. Admit fault when warranted. When someone blogs, tweets, or posts online about you, you may respond directly to the poster. Often they are seeking validation that a mistake has been made and just want something done to rectify the problem.

- **Address any errors, gaffes or blunders made by your company and explain**:
  - Why the problem occurred.
  - What will be done to fix the problem.
  - What will be done so it doesn't occur again.

It used to be a unflattering story would appear in the press and be forgotten after a few weeks or months. Today information posted on the Internet may never go away. So deal with online reputation disasters head on and stop it at the source.

Most online review sources will not remove negative posts unless they are obscene, racist, threatening, contain offensive content or otherwise violate posting guidelines. Reviews are very rarely removed once reviewed and approved. But that does not mean you are helpless to reduce the impact of negative reviews or comments. Take the following actions to protect your public image:

- **Ask the moderator to take a second look**. If you think the review violates the posting guidelines ask to have it re-moderated. Be specific and point out what is false, inappropriate or somehow violates the published guidelines.

- **Respond to the review quickly.**
    - Don't blame the commenter, even if you think they deserve it.
    - Never let a comment get under your skin.
    - Never post an emotional or accusatory response.
    - Respond in an appropriate and professional manner.
    - It is good policy to respond to all reviews on the sites most important to you.

- **Contact the reviewer directly.** Although reviews are often submitted anonymously, you may contact the reviewer directly through the website. To do this may require you have an account or membership on the site. Click the username on the review and then click "contact" on their profile page.

- **Solicit more reviews.** More positive reviews will push a poor review lower on the page and your overall rating will rise. Remember: "The solution to pollution is dilution." Zillow has data that shows the quantity of reviews drives more contacts to agents than the rating itself. Contact your clients and ask them to post. Email them a direct link to make it easier.

## Smartphone and Devices

Mobile phones are vital tools for real estate professionals, as important as a scalpel is for a surgeon. Mobile phones are designed for ease of use, but not for privacy and security. Not only can they fail to protect your communications, they also may leave you exposed to new kinds of privacy risk, especially location tracking. Generally, mobile phones give users less control than a full-sized computer, so it is harder to remove or replace undesirable apps bundled in with a desired application, and harder to prevent third parties from monitoring how you use the device. Smartphone vulnerabilities can be exploited, allowing others to:

- Listen in to your calls.
- Track your location using GPS.
- Look at your browsing history.
- Read your email.
- Exploit installed apps for banking, video camera systems, alarms and home automation systems.
- Spy on your Skype, WhatsApp or other messaging apps.
- Listen in over your microphone, even when you're not on a call.

Simple phone hacking instructions and a variety of hacking tools are easily found online. There are three primary ways to gain access to your phone; unsecured public wifi, unpatched operating system vulnerabilities, and malicious code. And once access is gained, remote access trojans (AKA:RATs) or other hostile programs are installed.

## Protecting Your Smartphone

You can never be 100 percent secure. But there are many ways to reduce the risk and make it harder for hackers to invade your smartphone. Here are some tips:

- If your phone warns you about the wifi hotspot you're trying to connect to, don't just click "ignore". Read the warning and weigh the risks.

- Turn off wifi and Bluetooth when not needed.

- Update your phone's operating system religiously.

- Limit the number of apps you choose to install. More apps equals more lines of code and therefore more exposure.

- Only download apps from trusted stores. Know who the developed the app.

- Look at the warning messages when installing applications.

- Lock your phone with a PIN or passcode.

- Set your phone to require unlocking if you don't use it for more than a few minutes.

- Have the locked screen offer a reward and display your (business) contact info.

- Back up your data regularly.

- Install, use and update a security and anti-virus program.

**Assume you'll get hacked sooner or later, probably sooner. Now what?**
The first step is admitting you are probably going to get hacked, even if you take all the right steps. If technically sophisticated Apple, Sony Pictures and even the Federal Government can fall victim so can you. Taking security precautions can defeat less sophisticated cyber criminals and slow down even the best ones, but you're never going to be 100 percent safe. The second step is being prepared.

- Monitor the news for emerging viruses, trojans, worms and other threats.

- Sign up for alerts from the US Computer Emergency Readiness Team (US-CERT) at www.ready.gov/cyber-attack

- Back up your data every day to a local drive and every week to either an online back-up service or to a removable drive you store off site or in a fire resistant safe.

- Set up system restore points frequently.

- Encrypt your sensitive data.

- Talk with your insurance agent about special cyber coverage.

- If you accept credit and debit cards you may be required to create a data breach Incident Response Plan. This plan should explain in detail the steps you will take should a data breach occur that exposes your customers' payment information.

- Consider keeping the computer with the most sensitive information disconnected from the Internet except when actually required.

**If you see signs a cyber attack is underway:** Take immediate action. This includes:

- Make sure the software on all of your systems is up-to-date.
- Run a scan to ensure your system is not infected or acting suspiciously.
- Disconnect from the Internet, by switching off your router or just unplugging the Ethernet cable.
- Restart your computer in the safe mode, then perform a full system restore.
- Change all your passwords right away. Prioritize by the potential harm.
- If sensitive information has been compromised, immediately notify all concerned including, staff, customers, banks, vendors and all of your online accounts. You may also need to alert the DMV and Social Security Administration if personally identifiable information has been accessed.
- Watch for any unexplainable or unauthorized charges or changes to your accounts.
- File a "Fraud Alert" with one of the major credit bureaus and review your credit reports.
- File a police report to document the crime.

## Working Safer Everyday

### Developing the Safety Habit

How are you going to remember all the tips provided in this book? Some of them might not be a good fit for you. Others are so common sense, and self-evident you've already internalized them. In any case, the purpose of this book is not to get you to commit the strategies, tactics and techniques to memory. Rather, the intent is to develop your awareness of factors that hazard your safety. Only by being aware can you make informed decisions about what level of risk you are willing to accept. Three to four weeks is all the time needed to develop such a habit. Then your new habit becomes automatic. The payoff is that once you develop the habit of being observant, choosing to pay attention to what is happening around you and asking "What if?" you will project an attitude of awareness and confidence that greatly reduces the odds you'll be targeted.

**Here are some ideas to help you make safety a habit-**

- Volunteer to become a safety advocate for your office and /or association.

- Bring up safety at meetings or ask that it be added as an agenda topic.

- Share safety tips by email, on your Intranet or on the break room bulletin board.

- Set up a Google or Topix news alert so you'll know how and where real estate professionals are being victimized.

- Keep a buddy system list of co-workers willing to tag along to meet prospects or sit at open houses.

- Make a game of being aware. Have colleagues and friends ask you at random times who is nearby, what they are doing, etc.

- Get to know the police in your area. Having a "friend on the force" can help you to be safe in many ways. Ask them to do a security audit on your office.

- Make updating software and passwords a high priority "To Do" item on your calendar.

- Have regular safety training classes focusing on self-defense, cyber security, and other safety related topics.

- Have a monthly safety tip contest.

### Recommended Safety Real Estate Safety Resources

**General Safety Tools**

Read or re-read "The Gift of Fear," by Gavin De Becker. This book will teach you how to be aware and use your intuition. Most libraries have it, but if yours doesn't buy it on Amazon or at a local bookstore. (This is listed first for a reason.)

These links to crime maps can help you stay on top of street crime in your area. If none of these cover your community, just Google "crime map and a zip code". www.spotcrime.com  www.mylocalcrime.com  www.crimereports.com

NSOPW is a U.S. government Website that links public state, territorial, and tribal sex offender registries from one national search site. www.nsopw.gov

**Real Estate Safety Tools**
The National Association of Realtor's safety page can be found at www.realtor.org/topics/realtor-safety
You'll find a variety of safety articles and videos there. The NAR has resources for associations and offices at www.realtor.org/topics/realtor-safety/resources-for-associations-and-brokerages

Best Defense USA offers a free sign you can print to help you get photo ID at open houses and other resources. http://bestdefenseusa.com/books_posters__reports

Join the Real Estate Agent Safety Forum on LinkedIn. This group is moderated by Tracey "The Safety Lady" Hawkins and is good place to share warnings, ideas and stories.

The Real Estate Safety Council is a nonprofit group of real estate industry leaders dedicated to improving safety in the workplace. Very good source for office forms, safety tips, and posters.
www.warealtor.org/safety-council

**Technology Safety Tools**
Security in-a-Box offers advice on how to use social networking platforms and mobile phones more safely. The Tool Guides offer step-by-step instructions to help you install and use the most essential digital security software and services. https://securityinabox.org/

"Have I been pwned?" is a free resource for anyone to quickly assess if they may have been put at risk due to an online account of theirs having been compromised or "pwned" in a data breach. It simple to use and entirely free. https://haveibeenpwned.com/

Want to see exactly how long it would take a hacker to crack your password? This link will do it.
https://howsecureismypassword.net/

This website offers a really big list of computer security resources. www.cyberdegrees.org/resources/the-big-list/

The National Cyber Security Alliance helps users at home, work and school with the information they need to keep themselves, their organizations, their systems and their sensitive information safe and secure online and encourage a culture of cybersecurity. https://staysafeonline.org/

## A CLOSING THOUGHT
You may live in a city, a suburb or a small town. You may be a real estate newbie or maybe you're a veteran. You could be male or female, old or young, black, white, brown or red. None of these characteristics matter when it comes to safety. **Because no matter who you are or where you are the single most important thing you'll do today, tomorrow and everyday is…**

**"Return Home Safely at the End of the Day!**

## True Crime Story # 1: Matthew Wilson

In March 2007, Wilson contacted a real estate agent and informed her that he was interested in purchasing a new home. The agent met Wilson at the real estate office and showed him several homes for sale over the next two days. On the third day, Wilson and the agent visited another home. During the showing, Wilson brought the agent into the basement and pulled out a gun. Wilson told the agent not to scream or he would kill her. Wilson then handcuffed the agent to a pole in the basement and demanded money. Wilson took the agent's wallet, cash, wedding ring, credit cards, and driver's license and told the agent that he knew where she lived and would come find her. Wilson then pulled down the agent's sweater, undid her pants, and touched the agent's breasts and genitals before sexually assaulting her. Wilson also told the agent he wanted to "screw" her. Wilson then placed a knife to the agent's throat, told her not to scream, and then left the home, leaving the agent handcuffed to a pole in the basement. The agent remained in the basement for several hours until she was discovered by her husband and another real estate agent.

Wilson pawned the agent's wedding ring in Tennessee and was later arrested in Texas **in a car with another female real estate agent.** At the time he was arrested, Wilson was in possession of the credit cards, business cards and driver's license of the real estate agent he accosted in March 2007. The vehicle in which Wilson was arrested also contained a receipt from the store where the agent's wedding ring was pawned and a BB gun pistol. Wilson's fingerprints were found in the home where the agent was assaulted and on the agent's business card case. The agent also identified Wilson from a photo lineup and again at trial.

Wilson was charged with first-degree robbery, felonious restraint, forcible sodomy, sexual abuse, and four counts of armed criminal action. Wilson represented himself at trial and testified in his own defense. A jury found Wilson guilty of first-degree robbery, forcible sodomy, felonious restraint, sexual abuse, and four counts of armed criminal action. Wilson was sentenced as a prior and persistent offender to two consecutive sentences of life, two sentences of 15 years imprisonment, and four sentences of 25 years imprisonment.

Wilson planned to continue preying on female real estate sales people. A search of Wilson's 1995 blue Ford Contour, found handguns, knives, a stun gun, handcuffs, leg irons, duct tape, rope and more than 30 real estate business cards, along with several real estate magazines and relocation guides. Photos featuring blond-haired female agents had been circled.

**ANALYSIS:** This real estate agent did the right thing in meeting Wilson at her office. However, Wilson was not pre-qualified and was not required to show a photo ID, but his name and license plate number had been recorded. After spending some time with him she became relaxed either because Wilson was not putting out any signals of his true intent or because she did not recognize them. Going into a basement by yourself, with a person not well known to you is a risky behavior. According to experts, one should never allow a person to restrain (tie up) them. Even if threatened with a weapon, running away and/or fighting back generally gives a better chance of escaping to safety.

**Disclaimer-** The purpose of this case study is not to blame the victim. Safety is a basic human right and is not forfeited by mistakes or carelessness. Clearly it is easier to see mistakes and opportunities in hindsight. It is hoped lessons can be learned to prevent future victims.

# True Crime Story #2: Ann and James

**THE FACTS:**
71 year old Ann Nelson was a Realtor, a wife, a mother of six, a polka dancer, and a churchgoer who made prayer shawls for the sick. Her March 2008 murder stunned South Central Wisconsin, especially the real estate community. Nelson was found dead in a smoke-filled room of a vacant home. Deputies found her body after her family called authorities and said she hadn't come home.

According to the criminal complaint filed in Jefferson County, Nelson, who worked as a real estate agent for RE/MAX Community Realty in Lake Mills, had an appointment with James A. Hole to show him a house just north of Lake Ripley in the Town of Oakland.

The six foot, two inch, 225-pound, Hole told investigators he met with Nelson to see property that he had not realized at first was only a lot with unimproved land. The agent then offered to show him a nearby property with a home on it. Nelson then showed him another nearby house. When the pair discussed price Nelson asked why Hole was looking at a home he wasn't planning to buy, the criminal complaint said.

"The next thing he knew, he was upset and strangling Ann Nelson," he admitted. Then he choked Nelson with her scarf and hit her at least twice with a fireplace poker, because she was screaming, "Help me, someone help me," and he wanted her to be quiet. The complaint states that he then became upset and strangled her.

After striking Nelson, Hole left the home, traveled a short distance and then realized he needed to destroy the evidence. His intention allegedly was to start the house on fire. He saw that Nelson was still moving and was conscious. He said he set a box of tissues on fire so he could use that to set the bed on fire, according to the complaint. An autopsy concluded Nelson died of smoke inhalation, but she also had head injuries, investigators say.

Hole was arrested after he was taken in for questioning. Records show he served more than eight years in prison in Illinois for aggravated criminal sexual assault before getting released. Hole also admitted taking a purse from Nelson's vehicle, taking valuables from the purse and hiding it in the house, where it was later found.

James A. Hole was sentenced to life in prison with no possible release.

**ANALYSIS:** Going alone to meet a stranger is an unnecessary risk. Not knowing the nature of the property he asked to see should have been a red flag. Ann was a smart woman who knew how to handle herself. But confronting a large man, while alone in an empty house, when it became apparent he could not afford the home may have been her downfall.

**Disclaimer-** The purpose of this case study is not to blame the victim. Safety is a basic human right and is not forfeited by mistakes or carelessness. Clearly it is easier to see mistakes and opportunities in hindsight. It is hoped lessons can be learned to prevent future victims.

## True Crime Story # 3 A Story of Survival

Veteran real estate agent Janice Tisdale survived an attack by a predator posing as a prospect. In an interview with ABC's "20-20" program the San Antonio Texas agent detailed the attack hoping to help others protect themselves from future threats.

Tisdale had developed a number of safety habits. She removed her jacket, made sure she knew the best escape routes at the property she was showing and unlocked doors to aid in escaping if need be.

She had agreed to meet Emilio Maldonado and his bank to show them a vacant, high-end home in a somewhat remote subdivision. As soon as she arrived at the appointment she noticed the banker wasn't there and it was just her client, Emilio Maldonado. "As soon as I pulled up I said, 'Where's your banker?' And he goes, 'Oh, he couldn't come today,'" Tisdale recounted for ABC News' "20/20." "And I thought, 'Oh, this is weird.' You know? It just didn't feel right."

Tisdale instincts were telling her to bolt. "The hair on the back of my neck was standing up, and I just was feeling really uncomfortable," Tisdale recalled. "And finally I said, we really need to go. So, we started out the door, and I reached down to pick up the lock box. That's when he struck me over the head."

Tisdale, badly hurt and bleeding, stood back up and boldly yelled out: "'Why did you hit me over the head?' And he just looked at me and he said, 'I need four thousand dollars.'" Maldonado held Tisdale hostage for 45 minutes. Tisdale channeled her former training as a flight attendant in remaining calm and continuing to talk to him.

"I just kept telling him, 'You just need to go to your car,'" Tisdale said. "'You need to get a piece of paper. I'll write that you did not attack me … and my husband will totally believe me, because he calls me such a klutz!'" Maldonado finally did go toward his car, and as he did, Tisdale ran off. But Maldonado ran after her. "My heart must have sank, and I just thought, 'You're dead, Janice. You are dead,'" Tisdale said.

Up ahead, Tisdale spotted teenagers driving down a road in a Honda Civic. She screamed for help, and yelled out "he's trying to kill me!" The teens slammed on their brakes to help. Tisdale believes the teens actions were responsible for saving her life.

Police arrested Maldonado shortly after. He was convicted and is serving 60 years in prison for aggravated robbery.

"I had drugs in me at the time, and that's what took my mind," Maldonado, now 76, told ABC's 20/20. "I sat there when I was looking at the house, and … my mind was going somewhere else. I just didn't realize what I was doing."

Tisdale says she will never enter a property alone anymore, and she always carries a hand gun. She realizes she was one of the lucky ones. In the past 10 years, more than 20 real estate agents have been murdered, according to the U.S. Bureau of Labor Statistics.

Disclaimer- The purpose of this case study is not to blame the victim. Safety is a basic human right and is not forfeited by mistakes or carelessness. Clearly it is easier to see mistakes and opportunities in hindsight. It is hoped lessons can be learned to prevent future victims.

## True Crime Story # 4  Armed and Licensed to Sell(Real Estate)

A Jonesboro Arkansas real estate agent was preparing to show a single-family home to a prospective buyer. She had shown the property a number of times over the last few months without any unusual encounters or signs that it was occupied. Then came the Friday evening when, having arrived before the buyer, she entered the home to await their arrival.

Upon entering she found two strange men inside the house. She drew her concealed weapon before ordering them, at gunpoint to go back into the room they had just left, but they fled instead. She then discovered a naked, unconscious man, later identified as Corey Lance Vandyke, face down on a bed. The real estate agent called the police, who arrived a short time later.

The responding officers ordered the suspects to come out of hiding. After the two suspects failed to respond to the officer's loud commands, entry was made into the locked bedroom where the suspects were thought to be concealed. However, apparently they had fled through the bedroom's window.

Vandyk was awoken and placed under arrest. He threatened the arresting officers, stating, he had a 22 rifle with iron sites that he was going to put between their eyes. He also told one of the officers he was going to put a bullet into the back of his head.

Officers searched the premises, collecting an unloaded rifle and a shotgun from the home. A marijuana plant was discovered growing in the backyard, was removed and logged into evidence.

There is no way to determine what would have happened if the real estate agent had not been armed or had hesitated to pull her weapon.

**Disclaimer-** The purpose of this case study is not to blame the victim. Safety is a basic human right and is not forfeited by mistakes or carelessness. Clearly it is easier to see mistakes and opportunities in hindsight. It is hoped lessons can be learned to prevent future victims.

## True Crime Story # 5- Realtors Defrauded Out of $2 Million Advertising Scheme

The following is taken from a FBI press release.

A Louisiana resident has been indicted by a federal grand jury in Pittsburgh on charges of mail fraud. The 11-count indictment named Rex Alan Harris, aka Michael Harris, Rex Rogan, Rex Alan, dba "Agents By City," 40, of Covington, La., as a defendant. The indictment was returned on April 19, and unsealed yesterday following Harris' arrest in Louisiana. His arraignment is scheduled for May 23, 2016, in U.S. District Court in Western Pennsylvania.

According to the indictment, since 2008, Harris defrauded hundreds of realtors nationwide whom he promised television and Internet advertising to generate home sales. Realtors were induced to pay thousands of dollars for advertising on major television networks based upon the realtors' zip codes. However, the advertising never occurred, and Harris and others spent the money for their personal benefit including purchases of tens of thousands of dollars in merchandise through PayPal, Footlocker and Nike.com, and New Orleans Saints season tickets, totaling in excess of $2 million.

Realtors who paid money to any of the following entities - "Our Family First Realty," "Better Realty Deals," "Amazing Realty Deals," "The Top Agent/Monolith Media Group," "American Real Estate Idols" or "Agents by City" - may be victims and are encouraged to call the Federal Bureau of Investigation (FBI) hotline at 1-800-CALL-FBI or 1-800-2255-324.

The law provides for a total sentence of 20 years in prison and a fine of $250,000 at each count or both. Under the Federal Sentencing Guidelines, the actual sentence imposed is based upon the seriousness of the offenses and the criminal history, if any, of the defendant.

Assistant United States Attorney Gregory C. Melucci is prosecuting this case on behalf of the government.

The U.S. Postal Inspection Service and the FBI conducted the investigation leading to the indictment in this case.

An indictment is an accusation. A defendant is presumed innocent unless and until proven guilty.

Disclaimer- The purpose of this case study is not to blame the victim. Safety is a basic human right and is not forfeited by mistakes or carelessness. Clearly it is easier to see mistakes and opportunities in hindsight. It is hoped lessons can be learned to prevent future victims.

## Real Crime Story #6- 30 Years in the Business a Few Minutes of Fear

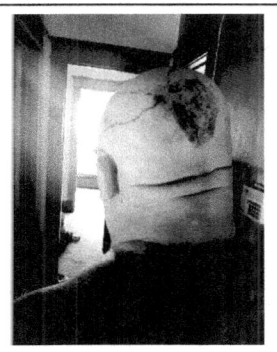

Jim Olsen shared this photo of the wound he received in the robbery.

Real Estate Agent Jim Olsen expected nothing more than a routine showing of a rental property to a prospective tenant. With thirty plus, more or less routine, years in the business, the 61-year-old agent had no reason to suspect he was walking into an ambush.

With his wife waiting outside in their truck, Jim went to meet the young, female prospect, who was waiting for him on the front porch. At first, the noontime apartment showing was routine, nothing appeared to be out of the ordinary. But then, as he walked towards one of the bedroom at the apartment's rear, a door flew open and a masked man with a gun stepped out to confront Olsen, while an armed and masked accomplice came out of the bathroom.

"It seemed strange to me that all the doors were closed. When I entered the kitchen, the door swung open and a gunman approached me and just stuck a gun right in my face and said "get on the floor," Olsen said to a local TV reporter. One of the men put a gun to the side of Olsen's head. "Then they whacked me in the back of the head. I fell to my knees. I got on the floor. They rifled through my pockets and asked me where the money was. "I feared for my life. I really thought that, laying on the floor, I was going to get shot in the head."

After ordering him to lie on the floor they pistol-whipped, before demanding money, which they took along with Olsen's smartphone, and wedding ring, before fleeing via the back door. Olsen left through the front door and returned to the truck where his wife called for help.

"I've been in this business for over 30 years and never have I feared for my life like I did that day," Olsen stated in a letter to other real estate agents.

"From now on especially with vacant homes and showing properties to unknown clients I will always walk around the house and make sure it is secure before walking in the front door."

"This was an eye opener. It was a shocker," Jim Olsen, 61, said in an interview with a Milwaukee newspaper. "It happened in the blink of an eye.

Disclaimer- The purpose of this case study is not to blame the victim. Safety is a basic human right and is not forfeited by mistakes or carelessness. Clearly it is easier to see mistakes and opportunities in hindsight. It is hoped lessons can be learned to prevent future victims.

## Real Crime #7- Attempted "Date Rape" at a Model Home

A real estate sales representative at a model home in North Carolina may have been the victim of an attempted drug facilitated sexual assault. The victim called authorities after experiencing an accelerated heart rate and numbness in her legs. After being transported by ambulance, to the hospital where doctors pumped her stomach she was able to recover quickly. A toxicology screen of her water bottle found traces of a date rape drug.

The male suspect first visited the model home about four days before the incident occurred. He began asking odd questions and would not give his name when requested to do so. The suspect returned the following Saturday at which time the sales rep was with a customer in the model home. After hearing the front door chime, she walked into the sales office inside the model home and saw the man in the vicinity of her desk.

At this time there was also a family looking at the model and the suspect said he would come back when the sales rep wasn't busy and then left abruptly. After the family departed the sales rep drank from her water bottle, which she had left, unguarded, on her desk." After about 20 minutes, she started to feel ill and called 911.

Drug Facilitated Sexual Assault (DFSA) is a sexual assault (rape or otherwise) carried out on a person after being incapacitated due to being under the influence of a mind-altering substances intentionally administered by another. In some cases, the victim willing consumes drugs or alcohol for recreational reason. In other cases the substances is surreptitiously introduced into a victim's drink. The victim will lose awareness of her surroundings and may remember little or nothing while under the drug's influence.

DFSA perpetrators tend to be opportunistic and non-confrontational. They prefer not to threaten, use force, or batter their victims. In most cases they do not carry weapons, steal or commit vandalism. They are not likely to have a history of physical violence. Perpetrators are often socially inept, living alone, with poorly established intimacy with others. As drugging a victim makes it possible to easily overpower them, it is possible for predators to commit a DFSA quite late in life, with perpetrators at age of 60 and older.

In addition to alcohol, common date rape drugs include rohypnol (roofies), ketamine (vitimin K) and gamma-hydroxybutyrate (GHB). These drugs have no color, smell, or taste making them difficult to detect.

To protect yourself from DFSA, never leave your beverage where it can be tampered with. If you think an unguarded beverage may have been adulterated discard it or store in a secure location for later crime lab processing. Never accept a drink from a person you don't trust. If you start to feel lightheaded, nauseous, dizzy or otherwise feel odd seek help immediately.

Disclaimer- The purpose of this case study is not to blame the victim. Safety is a basic human right and is not forfeited by mistakes or carelessness. Clearly it is easier to see mistakes and opportunities in hindsight. It is hoped lessons can be learned to prevent future victims.

**Real Crime #8-  He's Back!**

Only three years after charged and convicted of abduction in 2013, Robert E. Willett was released on June 11, 2016.  Previously, Willett had used at least 2 aliases, Bill Parks, and Tim Ramsey, when setting appointments with various realtors for house showings. He had also been seen loitering at open houses as well, where he would illegibly sign the register and then stayed to the end, being the last to leave. Realtors who have had encounters with Willett have all described him as "off," and stated that he made them feel uncomfortable. He is currently unemployed, but has previously represented himself as a firefighter and as a security officer. He was able to display badges for both. Real estate agents noted his disheveled appearance, and stated they didn't believe he could afford the properties he was inquiring about.

Willett has a long history of preying on female real estate professionals. One female agent has identified Willett as the prospective homebuyer who groped her in 2006.  Others say the six foot five inch, 280 pound predator has lingered too long at open houses.  Reports on file from 1999 and 2006 indicate Willett has a long term pattern of this type of behavior.  In 2010, police arrested Willett after he arrived at a showing with flex cuffs, scissors, and a knife on his person.

The 2010 arrest occurred after Realtor Jana Chervenic received a pornographic image sent anonymously to her cell phone.  "I was aggravated that somebody would do that in the middle of the night," she said. "So, I decided that I would keep that phone number and try to figure out who it was. "I wanted to be able to know what this person looked like. I wanted to know who he is because he knew who I was."

10 days later Chervenic got a phone call from the same number. The man wanted to meet with her to view a house.  The realtor contacted Akron police due to her feeling uneasy about Willett's behavior.
 She then agreed to help set up the sting that ended with Willett's arrest.

In 2013 Willett "bear hugged" a Realtor, resulting in a struggle between them. She was able to get free and drive away.  Willett was identified by DNA on a pop bottle he had left inside the Realtor's vehicle

Upon release Willett was placed on post release control with the Adult Parole Authority. As one of his conditions of parole, he is forbidden to have any contact or schedule any appointments with real estate agencies or Realtors. For the duration of his post release control (3 years) Mr. Willett will be placed on intensive supervision assigned to a US Marshall Fugitive Task Force Parole Officer. Parole will strictly monitor his activity and look for suspicious trends in his movement patterns.  Nevertheless, Willett will still be able to travel freely as it will be impossible for law enforcement authorities to know where and what he is doing at all times.

After only three years in a correctional facility Willett is now out and may well re-offend.  There is no reliable way to determine if a sexual predator has been "cured."  Sex offenders are always at high risk for committing future crimes.

Disclaimer- The purpose of this case study is not to blame the victim.  Safety is a basic human right and is not forfeited by mistakes or carelessness. Clearly it is easier to see mistakes and opportunities in hindsight.  It is hoped lessons can be learned to prevent future victims.

## Real Crime # 9- Open to Suspicion

Criminals typically target three items to steal at open houses- jewelry; handguns; and prescription medications. Or they may be looking to scope out opportunities for future crimes. The following stories are taken from actual police reports.

**Partners in Crime-** Real estate agent Linda Johnson was conducting an open house for clients in Clifton Heights, OH when targeted by a husband and wife criminal team. "He was telling me this story," Johnson explains. "The wife said, 'Oh, he's going to talk forever, so how about if I just go upstairs and take a peek?'"

Later that evening, when the client went to retrieve prescription medications from her nightstand and a number of bottles of pharmaceuticals were missing.

**Suspicious Person-** A Lake Forest, Illinois police officer responded to the 100 block of Ravine Forest Drive for a report of a suspicious person. The officer met with a local real estate agent, who was hosting a broker's open house. The agent said that a man posing as an agent came into the house and then went upstairs to look around. She stated she heard noises coming from upstairs and shortly thereafter the man came back downstairs and left. The same man also went to another nearby home and repeated the behavior. The man signed in using false names at both homes and apparently was never required to show proper identification. No items were reported stolen from either home but police believe he may have been casing the properties for a future burglary or other crime.

Disclaimer- The purpose of this case study is not to blame the victim. Safety is a basic human right and is not forfeited by mistakes or carelessness. Clearly it is easier to see mistakes and opportunities in hindsight. It is hoped lessons can be learned to prevent future victims.

## True Crime Story # 10: A Craigslist Scam

The popular website Craigslist offers a great resource for buying and selling, hiring employees, finding services and making social connections. But Craigslist also has a dark side.

In an interview with TV station WAAY, Huntsville Realtor Martella Tyler provided a cautionary tale of a scammer who took information posted online for one of her listings and posted a Craigslist ad posing as the owner looking to find a tenant to rent the property. Tyler learned of the attempted fraud when she received multiple calls from would be tenants interested in renting the home.

One of the callers even provided her with a false lease agreement. The scam artist also asked for a $600 down payment. "He was very interested and wanted to go ahead and get his keys and move in and pay his deposit and I explained to him that there is no deposit, the house is for sale," she said.

The Huntsville Police Department is warning the public about the potential dangers of Craigslist scams. "We have seen a number of cases. Some of it involves trying to purchase items with counterfeit money," says Lt. Darryl Lawson.

"I cannot believe this is happening. I've just never seen someone actually take someone else's product that they're selling and clone it and try and make it their own," said Tyler.

Craigslist is aware of scammers using their website to commit fraud. The web site has posted the following safety tips.

- Deal locally, face-to-face —follow this one rule and avoid 99% of scam attempts.
- Do not extend payment to anyone you have not met in person.
- Beware offers involving shipping - deal with locals you can meet in person.
- Never wire funds, e.g., Western Union - anyone who asks you to is a scammer.
- Don't accept cashier/certified checks or money orders - banks cash fakes, then hold you responsible.
- Transactions are between users only, no third party provides a "guarantee".
- Never give out financial info (bank account, social security, paypal account, etc.).
- Do not rent or purchase sight-unseen—that amazing "deal" may not exist.
- Refuse background/credit checks until you have met landlord/employer in person.

**Disclaimer-** The purpose of this case study is not to blame the victim. Safety is a basic human right and is not forfeited by mistakes or carelessness. Clearly it is easier to see mistakes and opportunities in hindsight. It is hoped lessons can be learned to prevent future victims.

**About the Author:**
"Joe Rosner is the Director of Best Defense USA and is a nationally recogized speaker on workplace violence, personal safety and self-defense, His credentials include military, law enforcement and bodyguarding, multiple black belts and growing up on the southside of Chicago. He is sought after presenter on topic related to active shooter and other forms of workplace violence.
He can reached at joe.rosner@usa.net